A French Restoration

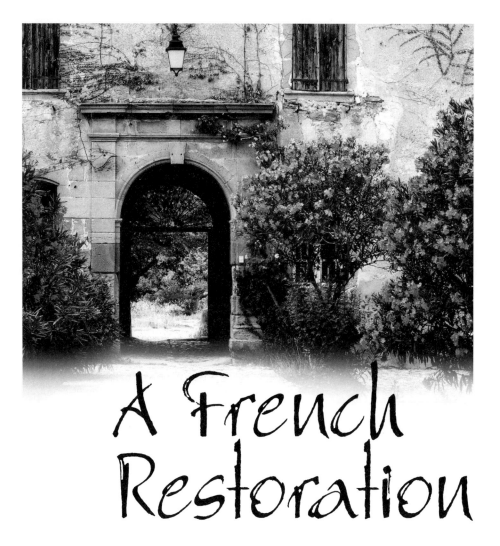

A French Restoration

The pleasures and perils of renovating
a property in France

CLIVE KRISTEN
and **DAVID JOHNSON**

how to books

Published by How To Books Ltd,
Spring Hill House, Spring Hill Road
Begbroke, Oxford OX5 1RX
Tel: (01865) 375794 Fax: (01865) 379162
email: info@howtobooks.co.uk
http://www.howtobooks.co.uk

Text © Clive Kristen and David Johnson

First edition 2006

ISBN 13: 978 1 84528 068 0
ISBN 10: 1 84528 068 7

British Library Cataloguing in Publication Data
A catalogue record for this book is available from
the British Library.

Produced for How To Books by Deer Park Productions, Tavistock
Typeset by *specialist* publishing services ltd, Montgomery
Cover design by Baseline Arts Ltd, Oxford
Printed and bound by Cromwell Press Ltd, Trowbridge, Wiltshire

Note: The material contained in this book is set out in good
faith for general guidance and no liability can be accepted
for loss or expense incurred as a result of relying in particular
circumstances on statements made in the book. The laws and
regulations are complex and liable to change, and readers should
check the current position with the relevant authorities before
making personal arrangements.

Contents

Part II The Practicalities

Photographs

Introduction

1 – THE REASON FOR THIS BOOK

Magazines with an interest in promoting the French property market cling to clichés such as: *'It was love at first sight'*, *'How we found our dream home'*, and even more improbably *'We never had a moment of regret'*.

And, to perpetuate this imbalance they rarely touch on:

- The dodgier sales methods of some estate agents.

- The pros and cons of using unregistered British builders.

- Language problems – using the telephone is the ultimate test.

- Health care – when top-up cover is essential.

- Taxation – with national and two levels of local tax to consider. And this does not mean you can escape the long arm of the Inland Revenue.

- Bureaucracy – the French have, *pro rata*, more paper pushers than any other nation on the planet.

- The resentment of communities to 'foreigners', particularly those who speak little or no French.

- How France's 'peasant economy' can benefit your lifestyle.

- How to adapt to life in France. Or, why one UK family in three sells up and returns to Britain within three years.

These seem, to me, to be pretty glaring omissions. In fairness, the better magazines, and certainly the broadsheet press, do run well-written articles relating to banking, health, taxation, and so on. But the advice is invariably, perhaps inevitably, generalised in a way that can become misleading. Our experience, at the blunt end, has often been *'that's not what we expected at all'*.

Take a visit to a French doctor. You know two things. Firstly, the EHIC (which you should have obtained in the UK) provides reciprocal free healthcare throughout the EC for yourself and your family. Secondly, the French health care system is superior to the NHS.

However, this helps little in practice. Go to a French doctor with a minor ailment and you get the full medical: heart, lungs, blood pressure, etc., as well as questions about diet, bowel movements and exercise. Then you get the prognosis for each of the leading English contenders in the Champions' League with pointed reference to the number of French players each English club has on its books. Finally, you will be given a prescription and a bill. Both of these mean you hand over a wad of cash up front. This may not be what you had anticipated, but it's the way it works.

According to your circumstances you may get some of your cash back. Eventually. Well, maybe. French healthcare is good, but expensive. It has created a financial black hole in the French economy. You pay your bills up front and you pay again in taxes. And it can only get worse.

Our plan was to buy and renovate an old building. We had limited funds, but had recently brushed up our DIY skills. But that was DIY UK and this can easily get lost in translation. If you don't believe it, take a closer look around a French builder's merchant. I could identify around half the products and make a fair guess at a few more. But a closer look did nothing for my confidence. Some things look the same but deep down they are different. Take French electrics. Very tricky. This leads to implications for safety, insurance, and imported electrical products. French plumbing is even more bizarre. Central heating, for instance, is driven by water pressure, not gravity. Pipe gauges and couplings are antediluvian – although a course in medieval architecture may just help.

Which takes us to the mystery of *la fosse*. We knew septic drainage was *de riguer* in rural France, but nothing of the etiquette associated with pumping out 3,000 litres of effluent. First, do not to rely on your neighbours' noses to inform you the tank needs emptying, but do give them due warning when the man with the pump truck is coming. The aroma, as they say, wasn't built in a day.

We estimated that the restoration, working alongside a local builder, would take three years. That was about the only thing we got completely right. And, as we could only afford to work on one area at a time, we had to prioritise. We decided that the kitchen came first, although that is not what happened at all.

Renovation does not come in discrete chunks. There is no point in digging up a floor for new cabling if three months later you are digging it up again to lay new water pipes. And, you don't know you need new water pipes until you have shifted tons of earth and concrete. And inevitably, as the roof is a lower priority, it will start to leak just as you have fitted your new units.

All this challenged our sanity. But there was a massive satisfaction too. I became fairly competent as a plasterer, a tiler, breeze blocker, ditcher, glazier, concreter, and gardener. Doris rubbed down everything else and painted it. We saved a small fortune, but with a more reliable builder we would have saved a large one.

This, then, is the story of two people, old and wise enough to know better, who bought and restored their own mini-chateau in the middle of *La belle France*. It is also the story of La Maison D'Etre herself – a property whose own character reflects her colourful past. Yes, we love her to bits.

If I was to write those magazine catch lines they would be *'Love at 16th sight'*, *'How we found our ruin'*, and *'Despite regrets and recriminations we would do it again'*.

David Johnson

2 – A RENOVATION STORY

In December 2004 Justin Ryan and Colin McAllister of *'The Million Pound Property Experiment'* said, 'We are entering an interesting time in home improvements. As increasing numbers of Brits are choosing to pay for time off and a quality finish, it seems that the thirst for DIY may be drying up'.

At the same time Standard Life Bank also claimed that more British men were hanging up their hammers. Indeed, it was estimated that during the previous year householders had spent an average of £4,500 on tradesmen rather than tackling jobs themselves. A more startling statistic was that British men were prepared to pay out a fifth of their take home pay to tradesmen in order to buy more spare time. Builders, plasterers and window fitters appear to have benefited most from this new trend.

But whilst the DIY stores in the UK have found life tougher – and have diversified accordingly – profits from *bricolage* and builders' merchants in France have never been greater. And yet there is no reason to believe that Frenchmen have suddenly begun to prefer DIY to football, rugby and *la chasse* (which sometimes may even include hunting). Indeed it is a phenomenon that the French themselves have not quite come to terms with, although there are clear indications that 'immigration' (which includes the 10,000 or so Brits who relocate to France every month) has something to do with it.

I believe this may be true. And with good reason. A lovely rural property surrounded by several green acres in, say, Brittany, can be purchased and renovated for a total of around €225,000 whilst a similar property and renovation in, for example, Oxfordshire, would cost at least three times as much – beyond most people's means and dreams. Or put it another way: in France it is possible through a renovation project – which may well include some DIY – to build for a superior lifestyle in which the principal beneficiary is not the bank or building society. The incentive therefore, to invest time, money and imagination in a project is also greater.

As soon as I heard that my old friends David and Doris Johnson had purchased La Maison D'Etre I was convinced that the unfolding story would be fascinating. I had worked with David before in bringing to publication his cycling adventures in a book that was to become *'Cycle Trails of the Yorkshire Dales'*. This time the idea of *'Renovating a Property in France'* seemed to sit naturally alongside titles I had already written for How To Books – *'Buying a Property in France'* and *'Buying to Let in France'*.

But we wanted to break away from the constraints of a fact-based manual. We wanted to help tell the unfolding story, as it happened, with the narrative method that we had developed for *'Cycle Trails'*. This meant, as far as possible, using David's own rhythm of words and anecdotal style. And for this to really work it had to be about much more than the process of restoration. We wanted to reach towards the soul of the property and the community in which it stood. Here there was history, tradition, a way of doing things, and even a way of thinking that is quintessentially French, albeit viewed through the irascible eyes of a dyed-in-the-wool Yorkshireman.

And there were also the characters. In the beginning the villains – the dodgy estate agents and builders – were invariably British. Here their identities have been as masked and shady as they are. Later though, perhaps when things were at their worst, it was the British community who rallied round to help complete the renovation of La Maison D'Etre. The French also have a pivotal role in the story. Here we see them as gregarious, elusive, infuriating, introverted, intriguing, beguiling, and most frequently charming.

I thank David for his massive efforts in working towards these aims. I also thank my wife, Maureen, for her contributions and suggestions. Most of all I thank Giles and Nikki of How To Books for committing to a project which stretches the boundaries of a publication style which has made How To the most trusted publisher of practical guides. I hope, in its own way, this title proves itself worthy to share the shelf space.

Clive Kristen

3 – A WORD ABOUT LANGUAGE

As a generalisation the French speak better English than the English speak French. In rural areas however the situation is more polarised. The French who speak English often do so to a high standard and like to practise it. There are some, however, particularly the older generation, who either have no English or simply refuse to use it.

When we have used speech in the narrative we have tried to reflect this. However, in order to make the language accessible to the reader we have generally limited French speech to well known phrases or those that will anyway be understood in context. Our primary aims have been to reveal character and to drive forward the narrative and the 'default setting' for speech, therefore, has necessarily been English.

That said, many of the conversations are not very far removed from their original framework. There are occasions, for instance, where you get 'Franglais' – the two languages mangled and improvised. This can occur for the best of reasons. Each person, out of respect perhaps, is trying to speak in the other's tongue. This is understandable, although it is likely that communication would be improved if each stuck to his own.

Equally it is easy to be misunderstood or misinterpreted through invalid assumptions about linguistic competence. We have all rehearsed stock phrases before going into a shop which encourages the person responding to the enquiry to mistakenly believe that you can also easily cope with a torrent of fast flowing French. Equally, you can be misunderstood by relying on 'false friends'. Words such as 'demand' and 'parent' have rather different meanings on opposite sides of the Channel.

Another problem is regional dialect. This is not specific to rural France but it is often in the rural areas where it is most influential and noticeable. In extreme cases it can be almost a *patois* which is only barely comprehensible even to native speakers of the French in the region. Imagine perhaps a Shetland fisherman talking to a Devon cattle farmer and you begin to get the idea.

It causes problems, but it is also the nature of linguistic diversity and we must celebrate it: it reflects culture, makes life itself more interesting, and is now and again the cause of great hilarity. *Vive la difference!*

The Authors

Photo 1 The authors (and friend) seated in the Odorat

Take more of your money with you

If you're starting an exciting new restoration project in France it's likely that the last thing on your mind is foreign exchange. However, at some point you will have to change your hard earned money into euros. Unfortunately, exchange rates are constantly moving and as a result can have a big impact on the amount of money you have to create your dream home.

For example, if you look at the euro during 2005 you can see how this movement can affect your capital. Sterling against the euro was as high as 1.5124 and as low as 1.4086. This meant that if you had £200,000 you could have ended up with as much as €302,480 or as little as €281,720, a difference of over €20,000.

It is possible to avoid this pitfall by fixing a rate through a **forward contract**. A small deposit will secure you a rate for anywhere up to 2 years in advance and by doing so provides the security of having the currency you need at a guaranteed cost.

Another option if you have time on your side is a **limit order**. This is used when you want to achieve a rate that is currently not available. You set the rate that you want and the market is then monitored. As soon as that rate is achieved the currency is purchased for you.

If you need to act swiftly and your capital is readily available then it is most likely that you will use a **spot transaction**. This is the Buy now, Pay now option where you get the most competitive rate on the day.

To ensure you get the most for you money it's a good idea to use a foreign exchange specialist such as Currencies Direct. As an alternative to your bank, Currencies Direct is able to offer you extremely competitive exchange rates, no commission charges and free transfers*. This can mean considerable savings on your transfer when compared to using a bank.

*Over £5,000

Information provided by Currencies Direct.
www.currenciesdirect.com
Tel: 0845 389 1729
Email: *info@currenciesdirect.com*

Part 1
La Maison D'Etre

1
Preparations

I was 68 years of age when I lost it completely. The wheelbarrow had already spilled hardcore left, right, and forward before we parted company. It accelerated down the plank way, lunged sideways like a cyclist after a liquid lunch, and emptied the remainder of its contents onto the floor of our kitchen.

Doris appeared with tea and bandages. She surveyed the scene. The dust swirled round the wheelbarrow, I was sitting untidily on the grass wiping soil and sweat from my eyes. I was also cursing loudly.

'I think that's enough for today,' she said, 'you're overdoing it again.'

'But we must be in by winter.'

'But if we're not, what's the worst that can happen?'

'We'll freeze to death in the caravan.'

'Yes, but it will be at least be peaceful. I mean, what will the postman think of us when you learn to swear in French?'

'Was he here just now?'

'Yes.'

'So what?'

'The 'what' is that the postman is also the Mayor. And, if the Mayor is upset, what happens to our planning permission?'

'I'd forgotten,' I said, 'oh *merde*'.

The slippery slope which led to my hardcore outburst had begun five years earlier. Doris and I had been married, although not always to each other, for the best part of fifty years. We had both been college lecturers – although not in subjects of massive practical use – and had ended up in Kent because the weather was better than Northumberland and most of our children had already migrated south.

We missed Northumberland; it has great swathes of wilderness and glorious golden beaches. But you don't splash around in the North Sea – even in summer – and come out a whole man. Kent was mellower but without the wilderness and miles of scenic sands. Ideally, we wanted to combine the best of both.

Although our careers had been only semi-distinguished we took great pride in our children – eight of them, plus a dozen grandchildren and counting. Here, we had done a decent job. In turn this meant that, though we were rich in life, our bank balances were humble.

As retirement approached we considered ways of bringing things together. In England, old people are politically invisible. Perhaps this is because governments believe the only things we would vote 'yes' to are higher pensions, bringing back Gracie Fields and the death penalty. Whatever the reason, which I suspect is mainly to do with the fact that we belong to a generation that doesn't make a fuss, we have the poorest health and smallest wealth in western Europe.

Worse still, England has become a place where the 'senior citizen' has become the 'old git' (or worse) and where the melody of life has become a thumping drum and bass. We have seen gangs of

4

youngsters hanging around shopping centre escalators, as damaged, derelict and threatening as the estates that spawn them. But we never see a parent, a policeman or a social worker. Like the old, these youngsters are always somebody else's problem. Britain has lost its self-respect. We did not want to lose ours. It was time to move on.

We thought about the Costa Del Gringos but rejected it. We had noticed that, as we became older, our body thermostats didn't work as well as they once had and, perhaps because of that, we had begun to enjoy seasons. We could do without a long winter but not perhaps without a faint dusting of snow and we wanted summer to be warm, but not so hot as to turn our legs to jelly.

Perhaps it was sipping the odd glass of Muscadet, but France seemed to loom ever larger in our thoughts. We were great Francophiles anyway, and so were many of the children. Once it had been camping. Then caravanning. There was not much of the country that we did not know and we liked most of it. That, in itself, created a problem: where should we go?

A villa in St.Tropez was not exactly us and, anyway, it was way beyond our means. Essentially we were looking for *la vie tranquille* in the rural France that was not running, so much as limping, into the 21st century.

The property would have reasonable access from the autoroute network. It would have to be far enough south to enjoy a decent year-round climate. It would have more potential than pretension and it would have to be large enough to accommodate our family in holiday 'shifts'. The garden would also have to be large enough to pitch tents and also be suitable for children to play safely.

Like most buyers, when it came down to it, the prime considerations were location and affordability. As far as location was concerned we crossed out the whole of France north of the Loire, the approaches to the Alps and Pyrenees, the Massif uplands and finally most of western France and Brittany on climatic grounds. Then we ruled out pretty much everything south of Angoulême on the grounds of either access or cost. Our target area was narrowing.

We also looked at conversion and renovation costs in general terms. We were aware that turning lofts and outbuildings into guest accommodation could be potentially pricey, however our wish list indicated that we would require at least three permanent double bedrooms and perhaps other smaller areas that could be adapted as temporary bed-space when the occasion arose. We would need lounge and dining areas large enough for a dozen or so people to munch and mingle without locking elbows, a proper kitchen area with breakfast space for six, an indoor zone where children could be stupefied watching Disney on DVD, some office and bookshelf space, and up to three bathrooms or 'wet areas'. Outside there would have to be secure parking for at least three cars, a caravan or two, and perhaps the occasional motorhome. There had to be space for children's slides, swings and paddling pools and an *aperitif* and barbecue area. A few shady trees and some designated produce areas – to grow whatever came to mind – would also be desirable. We were looking at a pretty substantial rural property.

We amassed material on local climate and property prices. We subscribed to French property magazines. We also read the very best books on the subject. This, of course, included 'How To Buy Property in France'. We hoped, for instance, that by being up to speed on key planning matters we could potentially avoid a few headaches. I recall wrestling with the notorious coefficient of building which indicates how much of a terrain could built on. There are also other national rules which apply to what you can and cannot do living close to, or even within line of sight of, a '*monument historique*', and the possible local governance which can affect matters such as 'change of use' applications. I rapidly forgot most of the detail, but retained a general understanding of the way to approach planning matters if I hoped to get a result.

We also came to an understanding that, for us, moving to France would mean more than adapting to a new language and culture. It would also mean making the most of rural life. This, in itself, would mean adapting to a lifestyle that would be very different from the Suburbia UK way of doing things. And it was going to be more than that. All our reading indicated that 'rural' in France means something more for most people than it does in the UK. Although it was clear the French were wrestling with problems that have destroyed communities in Britain – schools and shops closing, more rural crime, more second homes and *gîtes* and an influx of 'foreigners' who may not share local values – it remained clear that whilst a village in Oxfordshire was likely be more commuter than community, for the French the commune was still just one stage removed from the family. We had been surprised to learn, for instance, that if a complaint is made about a cat mewing late at night, the mayor is duty bound to investigate.

We had already determined that a substantial house in a village community would be ideal. Anything too isolated, even with solid doors and shutters, could be an easy target for crime. Much better to have local people walking by and ultimately, perhaps, the kind of good neighbours who know your routine – when you go to bed, when you are likely to expect visitors, etc. We have always felt that this brings greater peace of mind than elaborate alarm systems and all risks insurance.

I had read of a simple experiment: at a village – one of several claiming to be at the very centre of France – a large stone house stands next to a modern brick-built *pavillon*. The stone house stood, unheated, at around seven degrees in mid December and took three days to warm up to 17 degrees. The brick house started at nine degrees but warmed up to 20 in four hours. In mid July the situation reversed. The stone house started at 16 degrees and, when windows and doors were thrown open, edged cautiously up towards 20. The brick house started at 17, but, once the windows were open, the temperature soon hit 28.

The downside of stone was therefore that the property would take ages to heat through on a winter weekend, but that was not important to us as we intended to live there. Ultimately the stone would become be our friend. Once heated up it would retain its warmth, and in the summer the house would be deliciously cool. We even closed our eyes and imagined the chill of the flagstone floor on our bare feet on a scorching summer day. Stone seemed very much the way to go, particularly as it seemed to offer a possibility of renovating, at least in part, with reclaimed materials. We also liked the idea (at least) of restoring a vernacular building to something approaching its former glory. We were, though, still prepared to be seduced, at the right price, by an irresistible pile of bricks: we wanted to keep our options open.

We began our personal preparations earnestly: I took evening classes in plumbing, plastering and bricklaying and, although my conversational French was still only adequate, I gained some confidence through coming to terms with the technical language that would help me through the nuances of French septic drainage. We further developed our linguistic skills through a programme known as *Accelerated Learning*. As you approach 70 there are still some things that need to be learned quickly.

'*Accelerated Learning*' for us mainly meant getting together with the like-minded and punctuating an evening's *conversation Français* with *baguettes* and Brie washed down with a couple of bottles of Pays de L'Aude. It was tough but we battled on.

I am glad that we did. There can be no doubt that the main reason why the British fail to adapt to life in France is the language. On holiday you can fumble around with a few phrases and extravagant gestures. It's even quite fun to see just how much you can wing it. But, as time goes by, this becomes an irritation. Later on it can even become a nightmare: it keeps you out of the social loop, it keeps you out of the system. This applies even more to the telephone where you have no clues as to expression and body language.

This can be overcome with practice, but I admit I still avoid the telephone whenever I can. Two years on I still make my doctor's appointments in person, and before the visit to the surgery I rehearse any phrases I may need such as '*I can't sleep because of the late night mewing of Chatanova – the neighbourhood tom cat*'.

Perhaps the greatest difficulty with spoken French is that every noun has a gender and they like you to get it right. For a nation, however, that prides itself on rationality the logic of gender is totally irrational. A *gendarme* is masculine but the *gendarmerie* itself is feminine. *Prostate* is feminine and what my Pocket Oxford Dictionary defines as 'part of the reproductive system of most female mammals' is masculine.

The written language avoids the embarrassment of this problem but has pitfalls of its own. Official language can seem to be convoluted, but it is also very precise. Until recently, French has been the official language of diplomacy. We have learned to be wary of 'false friends' – words which seem to be similar to English, but have very different meanings: a letter from the water board saying they are coming to renovate *your* furniture applies to your drains not the sideboard.

During these months of preparation we were also talking to several UK based estate agents who had fingers in the French property pie, and came to realise how important it was to put the pieces of the financial jigsaw together before we went shopping. So, we looked carefully at our savings and pensions and tried to work out how far they would stretch in terms of our desires. The answer was that we could do it, but we would have to take care. There would not be a lot of cash to spare so we could not afford many mistakes.

2
House Hunting

In May 2001, we went to the French Property Exhibition in Harrogate. It was comprehensive, with strong representation from agents involved in France. I felt that one of them – let's call the company *Les Maisons Formidable* – looked impressive on their stand, but posters and embossed paper are easy enough to produce and, like an Armani suit, are primarily intended to impress. I knew we had to dig deeper – to find out what the operation looked like stripped to the raw.

Early the following year, 18 months before Doris planned to retire, we made an appointment to visit their London office near Canary Wharf; the premises were trim and tidy without the worst excesses of floribunda and Vivaldi. We had an interview with Justin – one of the directors – who helped us to make decisions in principle about areas of France which matched our aspirations and price range. This led to a potentially busy itinerary looking at property around Deux Sevres, the Limousin and the Charente.

But what impressed us most about *Les Maisons Formidable* was that this was a *'one stop service'* that dealt with every aspect of the purchase process. Included in the package was advice on rights of way, land divisions, and similar legal minefields. We were also promised that someone from the company would *'pop round for a cup of tea'* once we had settled in and give us the benefit of their experience of setting up a profitable *gîte* business or a bed and breakfast operation. On these – and other matters that could ultimately help us to make ends meet – more formal legal advice and aftercare was also to be made available. *Les Maisons Formidable* seemed just the thing for us.

At Easter 2002 we sailed for France towing our geriatric caravan to the municipal site in Deux Sevres. We had a couple of relaxing days in the sunshine, studying the specifics of our itinerary and mentally preparing for the whistle stop tour of 'suitable' property. We had just two weeks before Doris was due to return to work.

Day one started badly: we drove in ever decreasing circles on ever deteriorating roads until we ended up at a no-through hedgerow. Doris's eyes are better than mine and she spotted a ramshackle farm building on the horizon. All we had to do now was to find the road.

We turned around. Some little way back down the lane we watched a large lady close a field gate behind a geriatric 2CV; she took particular pains to hitch down her skirt and climbed into the vehicle. We watched as the little car ascended a track which could well have been used for tank training. The driver evaded the worst of the potholes, whilst the vehicle trampolined gently but resolutely through the dips which could not be avoided. I could not help contrasting this with Surrey stockbrokers' wives who drive their armoured personnel carriers daily, but test their off road pedigree just once a year whilst transporting sandwiches for the village gymkhana.

As the 2CV neared the farm building we knew that this must be our route. We parked our car tight against the hedgerow and followed on foot.

At the entrance to the farm buildings a 'for sale' sign indicated that this was the correct address. We knocked at the door. There was no response. Then, the same woman who had tested the 2CV's suspension appeared from behind a barn and explained that she had come to feed her horses.

11

'But is there anyone here?' I asked.

'Sometimes yes,' she said, 'and sometimes no. Today it is no, I think.'

It was now half an hour after our appointment time and there was no sign of the agent.

I used my mobile to telephone the office in London.

'Tarquin speaking.'

'Good morning Tarquin. What time is it?'

He hesitated. 'Nine o'clock?' he ventured.

'No, here in France it is ten o'clock.'

'And you have a viewing appointment?'

'Well done, Tarquin. Yes, for half past nine.'

'Ah.'

'And here we are ruminating, like the cows, in a field in Deux Sevres. It's attractive but aromatic. It would have been more instructive to view the property.'

'Ah, quite so.'

He took our details and promised to call us back. He didn't. Three further phone calls to the UK met with a similar wall of inertia.

Our next appointment was three days later. This was in the Limousin and we were also to view property nearby in the Charente. A campsite was booked by Anne and Ian – who had recently taken over *Les Maisons Formidable* regional office – that could serve both purposes. Anne even made an appearance *'just to see how things are going'*.

There must have been something in our demeanour – perhaps it was the way we were sticking pins into a doll dressed in estate agent pinstripes – that told her that we were a touch disgruntled.

'You look a touch disgruntled,' she said.

'*Beaucoup* pissed off in fact,' I said.

'Ah,' she said. 'I'd better ring London.'

She passed on apologies from a director called Jeremy and an assurance that we would receive '*top treatment*' from now on.

'And we have more than 600 properties on our books in the Limousin,' said Anne.

'Just as long as we don't have to look at all of them,' said Doris. 'I'd lose the will to live.'

A new, even busier, schedule was lined up. One for the following day; two the day after and three the day after that. Their plan was to use fatigue to force us into a decision.

Anne had arranged for us to liaise with a local agent to take us round the first batch of properties. We followed the directions to the agent's office and unerringly navigated our way to another hedgerow. I performed a nifty nine point turn and we drove slowly back up the lane until Doris spotted the mill building. The agency sign suggested that we had found the correct address. Again we parked the car tight against the hedgerow. It was 9.30. We were bang on time.

Here there was no rutted track to navigate – just a gate rusted shut on its hinges and a low slung cur (possibly a Doberman Dachshund) beyond. The dog's yellow toothy smile said 'come in and make my day'.

An attractive young lady appeared alongside the beast.

13

'The dog, is it safe?' I asked.

She spoke the kind of Franglais that I had previously thought was invented for Inspector Clouseau.

'You Engleash?'

'Yes.'

'He iz good dog. He like the chealdren.'

'Children?'

'Yes, chealdren.'

'Has he ever eaten a whole one?' I asked.

'An ole wern?'

'*Mais oui, un enfant entier…*'

'*Monsieur?*'

'*Est-ce que il a mangé un enfant complet?*'

She hesitated for a moment. The light dawned. She had seen the flaw in my argument. Or French.

'*Non, Monsieur,*' she said, '*si le chien mange tout l'enfant, c'est le chien qui est complet…*'

We started to laugh at the same time. It was Doris who explained that we had an appointment with the agent. The young lady lifted the gate so it swung open just enough…

'Come with me,' she said, '*et oubliez le chien. Il est,* how do you say… *un lache…*'

'A coward,' volunteered Doris.

'Yes, a cowhard. He iz biting only the purstman.'

She took us into the ramshackle mill building that served as an office and found old green polypropylene chairs for us in an alcove near the toilet. Through an adjacent hatchway we could see the agent, an older woman in a white linen suit, making notes in response to a stream of messages on her answering machine. When she had finished she began waving her arms which was our signal to enter the room.

'So many people now,' she said, looking significantly at the machine, 'wanting to buy the houses in France. It is crazy. Now tell me what it is you want?'

We had discussed our requirements in England and again at the regional French office of *Les Maisons Formidable* in France. Anyway, hadn't our initial schedule already been arranged? I was surprised that she did not have the paperwork.

'We are looking for a substantial detached rural property that requires renovation. The plan is to work alongside a local builder to bring things up to standard. We have more time than money and lots of children and grandchildren.'

Madame L'Agent looked bemused.

'There are not many detached properties in France,' she said. 'We are friendly people. We like to have close neighbours. You understand?'

We understood, although her contention went against everything we had observed in more than 30 years of visiting the country. In rural France, in particular, we had formed the impression that people liked space. Lots of space. After all, wasn't there four times as much space to go round *per capita*, and didn't a large proportion of those same *capitas* live in large towns and cities? Conversely wasn't it just the British who had become the semi-detached nation of Europe? And wasn't that the very essence of our reason for escaping the UK?

15

Perhaps we looked confused. But *Madame L'Agent* was determined to make sure that we were on message.

'We like to be very close,' she said, 'with each other.'

I had once seen a similar form of words advertising a French film.

'But we don't like to be close,' I said. 'We're British.'

'Very well,' she said, 'I will have a look in my drawers.'

Doris squeezed my hand tight enough to wipe the smile from my face and *Madame L'Agent* dug into a filing cabinet and produced a sheaf of paper.

'Here are nine possibles,' she said.

We perused the paperwork. Four of the properties did not remotely meet our requirements and one was very 'iffy'. This left us with four. She picked up a telephone, spoke brusquely, and within moments the girl we had encountered with the Doberman Dachshund came into the room.

'My daughter Amelie will show you,' said *Madame L'Agent* who immediately turned her attention back to the answer phone.

Amelie did not possess her own car; this, she explained, was because she was a student and could not afford the insurance. I wondered how this matched the claim that *'all viewings of property must be accompanied by a fully trained professional agent'*. But no matter, Amelie was, at least, a cheery companion. And even if she wasn't quite Liz Hurley (as in stop the traffic and watch cars run into the back of each other) gorgeous, she was sufficiently attractive to make me all but useless as a navigator. Keeping my eyes on the road was the best I could manage, Doris and Amelie shared the navigation duties: one with local knowledge, the other with a map.

At the first property Amelie could not find the key holder; property two required more resurrection than renovation and property three was a clerical error.

I should have known something was wrong – we found property three without a single three point turn. Tall silvered wrought iron gates led to a landscaped drive and garden. The house was porticoed with a patio and pool at the front and a tennis court set to one side.

Amelie, who knew our financial clout was limited to £50,000, was embarrassed.

'Tell them we'll take it without looking,' I said.

'I think we have come to the wrong place,' she said.

The right place was a kilometre further on. The main building was constructed of weathered concrete – part grey and part green. This was, Amelie explained, because the imbedded mosses had been less successful in taking hold in areas that enjoyed direct sunlight. Her assessment was probably correct. Sunlight had also kept the damp patches on the sunny side to a minimum. Round the back the walls oozed gently to about half way up, and running from beneath the rotting window frames, were soggy stalactites of something that resembled unpasteurised Brie.

We were aware that dilapidation can lend a kind of charm. The trick, we had read, was to look past it for possible serious defects. But we were thinking more about a ramshackle roof, mosses overhanging gutters and the odd patch of flaky paint. This place had all the allure of the lifers' block on Devil's Island. However, as we had come so far, we were determined to take the tour.

The property was as appalling inside as out. The kitchen smelt of rotting rubber which we put down to the antediluvian linoleum. The entire upstairs held the aroma of camphor – probably the legacy of a thousand mothballs.

'And where's the toilet?' asked Doris.

Amelie dutifully went in search of the phantom convenience, but we already knew what the outcome would be.

'*Je regrette Madame…*'

'But this information,' I said, waving the printed sheet at her, 'said that the place was habitable. Without a toilet?'

'I think,' she said, 'that there has been *un erreur…*'

Property four was a run down 1970s *pavillon*. It was utterly soulless and in the middle of nowhere and, judging by the sparks that were generated every time we threw a switch, it needed rewiring. It would also need some plumbing once the chocolate-toned bathroom suite had found its way to the tip. Otherwise we could have moved in the next day. But it would have been difficult to live with the present owner's taste in garden ornaments: Snow White was more than a touch provocative and the seven dwarfs were all endowed in a way that compensated for their lack of stature. Happily they were almost camouflaged by weeds.

It took an hour to drive Amelie back to the mill, and it took us a further two hours (in pretty much the direction from which we had just come) to get back to our camp site.

Our background reading had led us to believe that the principle sales ploy of French estate agents was charm. It began with a big smile and the sort of French accent you can cuddle, then there would be *petit fours* and coffee and the odd glass of bubbly. There would be references to the Greatness of Britain and the good taste and perspicacity of its mature citizens. Transport would be laid on in a vehicle in which even the climate control could not entirely mask the tang of soft new leather, and there would be Fauré and Dérufle on the CD changer, a cold drinks cabinet without Virgin cola, and a satellite internet system for clients to check their share portfolios.

I have heard it really can be like that, but not in the Limousin. This is the doss house end of the French property market: cheap and cheerful. Well, cheap anyway.

Estate agents have never featured in my top ten 'useful occupations' list. In the first place they could never claim to be either productive or necessary. The instinct therefore is to treat them like car salesmen: never look too keen, ask difficult questions, kick the tyres. But this wasn't going to work here: you don't kick tyres when the exhaust pipe is certain to crush your toes. And questions like 'does it have a toilet?' are not seriously probing. Let's face it: 'toilet' is just about as basic as 'steering wheel'. You assume it exists and hope it works. And as for not 'looking too keen', well that's easy, there's not much to enthuse about in a scrap yard.

But what made it difficult was that Ian and Anne were not like estate agents. It may have been because they were young and inexperienced but, whatever it was, they retained some uncharacteristically human qualities. Indeed, that same evening they came round to see how we had got on.

'You look a touch disgruntled,' said Anne.

'My gruntles are sore,' I admitted. 'I've spent around five hours in the car today and have not seen a remotely suitable property.'

Ian produced a bottle of Pineau. 'This will make things feel better,' he said. 'And we will find you a suitable property, and it could just be tomorrow. I have a list and we will come with you this time. After tomorrow though it will be someone else. We're off to Limoges for a couple of weeks. It's a basic training course for the job. But don't worry, somebody will help you find the right place. Eventually.'

Perhaps it was the thought of losing Ian and Anne that concentrated our minds. More likely it was because they had done their homework. All the properties we saw were worthy of consideration and the last one we viewed was like a sardine to a pelican: it fitted the bill perfectly.

The house was in the village of Entrechoux – several kilometres from the market town of Paroisse sur Charente. We had visited Paroisse before and we felt it had a certain charm but, more importantly it had doctors, chemists, bakers and restaurants – just about everything you need when playing the senior circuit.

Entrechoux is a traditional rural French village – proudly dressed in stone and grey pantiles, more conformist than *chic* and now a touch threadbare since being stripped of almost all commerce. A stream divides the village north and south. By the south bank the Romanesque church marks the geographical and spiritual centre. In front of the western door is a small but manicured village green (featuring the village pump, *lavabo*, and war memorial) flanked by shady limes. A few paces further to the west was a packhorse bridge which still carried all traffic bound up and down the main street.

A most substantial house stood sentinel by the bridge with a garden running down to the south bank of the stream. The property had clearly been prosperous – there were signs of extensions as well as a large double barn.

Although in massive need of attention there was something sensible and solid about it. It also had the presence of a prime location, like a mini-chateau. This had surely once been the residence of someone significant, and it was available for £20,000.

I had that feeling, it was like the inevitable consequence of spicy food and strong wine: you know what will happen if you do, but then what is the point of going to the restaurant if you don't? Doris clearly felt the same.

'Could this be it?' she said.

I squeezed her hand.

'I hope so,' I said.

Photo 2 Entrechoux with La Maison D'Etre on the right and
L'Odorat in the foreground

3
The Builder

'There is an excellent local builder,' said Anne, 'and he's English.'

'But that would leave us with a maximum of £30,000 to sort it all out,' said Doris. 'I like it but I'm not sure...'

'Give us time to think,' I said.

We had been told that there were rules of thumb for restoration costs in France. Three quarters of the purchase price was generally regarded as top whack, and, even if you buy a bare shell (roof, walls, window and doors) the cost shouldn't exceed the purchase price. Although we were aware that this would be subject to regional variation it was perhaps as good a starting point as any. On that basis – with £20,000 as a likely maximum for the project – we could just be in business.

'I could see if the builder is available now,' said Ian, 'just to give you an idea of costs.'

We should have held back. Why was our luck suddenly changing so quickly? But how could it be wrong to seek advice from a builder? He would obviously know more than we did. So what did we have to lose? We were only asking for an opinion.

After all our earlier frustrations, it must have been prescient that the builder, Kevin, happened to be on his lunch break. By a remarkable coincidence he also happened to be the husband of *Madame L'Agent.*

Photo 3 Entrechoux with Romanesque church, centre, and
La Maison D'Etre, left

He went round the property with us biting into a baguette. He had a pencil behind one ear, a Gitane behind the other, and a slim note book in the back pocket of his Wranglers. Consequently, his comments on the condition of the building were almost less interesting than watching his technique of juggling food, tobacco, and note-making without misadventure. I reckoned that anyone with such *savoir faire*, particularly as he never stopped talking, must be an at least competent workman.

He began with the outside.

'Look at the condition of the drainage channels round the walls. In most of these old houses the walls go straight into the ground – no damp course and no foundations. But, if most of the water is dispersed, it's OK. The rest of the damp climbs up from the ground, but again this doesn't have to be a problem as long as there are no cracks in the pointing. Then look for bulges in the walls or anything out of true. Bulging walls are bad news – especially high up, it means your roof is on the way down.'

'And look for damp patches. It could mean that there may be loose or cracked joints in the stonework; when the pointing comes away, the damp goes in. Our worst enemy is ivy. You know that the roots are going to pull out whatever they can and you can't tell how bad things are until you cut it back. I've seen walls collapse when the ivy is cut. Virginia creeper and clematis aren't as bad, they hang on somehow without eating into the mortar.'

'I have known Brits who look at an old roof – all bulgy and uneven – and think it is part of the charm of the property. But there's nothing charming about leaks, draughts and termites. When we go inside we will look for woodworm, but if the timbers are OK, the roof is probably OK.'

We followed him as he circumnavigated the property like trainee doctors in the wake of a celebrated surgeon on his rounds.

Finally, he cleared his throat and smiled.

'Could be worse,' he said. 'Now let's have a quick look round the garden.'

'What are you looking for now?'

He continued his commentary on the hoof.

'Well, you've got the river. If it floods, the garden washes away and the house will eventually follow, but I don't see any sign of that. I also look to see if trees have been taken out. If you chop down a tree it changes the natural drainage. I know a bloke who cut down half a dozen trees to make way for a tennis court; it was always wet. Should have put in a swimming pool.'

'And the roots from large trees can spread under your walls. We call it 'Billy Connolly' because it always brings the house down. Also look for cracks in the ground, they don't have to be big. When people put up extensions it can all get uneven. Different levels you see. When that happens you see cracks or mud patches between the new bit and the old, but I think your barn was put up at the same time as the house. There don't seem to be any problems here. Can we go into the house now?'

He had finished his baguette and poured himself a coffee from a thermos he had left on a low wall by the barn. He checked his notes quickly, tucked the pencil behind his ear and lit another cigarette. This was the signal for us to move on.

'We start off by looking for the dreaded damp,' he said. 'It hides itself behind panelling and plasterboard. The bastard. So what we do is look at skirting board height for mould. We also have a good sniff. When a house has been empty for a while there's always some damp. You'll often see patches on wallpaper. That's not too bad. When it's bad it peels off.'

He stopped and hesitated.

'Uh huh,' he said, 'look down here.'

He was now staring at an area on top of a skirting board. He ran a the little finger of the hand that held the cigarette along the top of the board and then lifted it to his nose.

'Musty you see. Do you want to smell?'

We declined. It is sometimes best to accept someone at their word. It shows you have faith in them.

'Is this a problem?' I asked.

'Not necessarily. You'd expect a bit of damp in a house like this. It's easily sorted. We just strip back to the stone and put in some *mortier bâtard*.'

'Bastard mortar?'

'It's a sand and cement mix with some of builder's friend – lime. The French use it for everything. If it's lime wash for the outside walls it's called *badigeon* or *chaux*. There are lots of different mixes.'

'It's cheap, freshens things up nicely, and covers a lot of sins. An extra little dab or two in a hole or crack? Who's to know? And better still it keeps the rain out but lets condensation escape.'

I was beginning to wonder where he had learned all the tricks of his trade when I was surprised to discover we could also count mind reading amongst his many skills.

'Before I came out here 14 years ago I worked for a UK outfit called Bodgitt, Shaftem and Scarper. No, I'm only joking. But they do exist, honestly. They're actually a reputable outfit. Blackpool or Cleveleys I think.'

'They'd have to be good with a name like that,' I said.

'Unless, of course, it's a double bluff,' said Doris.

'I don't think so,' said Kevin who immediately continued the tour.

'I'm pretty sure there's a *vide sanitaire* under this boarded living room floor. That's good news. It helps with air flow – cuts out damp and stops the joists from rotting. So let's go upstairs. We may not be able to see much of the roof joists – they'll be hidden by more floorboards, but we'll do our best. Remember to look out for woodworm.'

We followed him cautiously up the rickety stairs.

'We'll need some new treads here,' he said, 'don't worry, that's nothing. And yes, I was right, we can't see the roof timbers because of the boards. But look at the size of the beams going up. Know why that is? In the old days they used to shovel in buckets of earth as insulation. Works better than rockwool but it's heavy. The good news is that it means the house was built properly. Built to last. Not like modern houses. OK, so let's go downstairs.'

The house obviously had massive potential. It also, more or less perfectly matched our requirements. There were just two more questions.

'But how much will it all cost?' asked Doris.

'And how long will it take? I asked.

Kevin carefully dislodged a piece of salami skin from a tooth and lit another cigarette. Then he moved his head from side to side in the manner of the Old Bailey weighing scales. Finally he spoke.

'Ball park figure? I could firm things up later. Well, let's see. Rewiring and plumbing; new walls up, old walls down; new boards here; new boards there; some windows and glazing; some pointing and plastering; new kitchen units; bathroom suite. 'Course it depends what you want to spend there. Keep it simple and it shouldn't be too bad. You don't want gold taps do you?'

I shook my head. Gold taps were not part of the equation.

'Well, let's see. I reckon, with you working alongside me, around 15K should do it. 20K tops. Once we get really up and running we should get most of the work done in three to four months. So what do you think? Are we going to make this *un maison magnifique*, or what?'

His estimate was more or less exactly the figure we had hit on earlier. And it was just what we had hoped for. Was this serendipity or stupidity?

Doris and I looked at each other. She smiled. We both knew he had us.

'You'd be able to start when we need you?'

He nodded.

'Then we'll take it,' I said.

4
Formalities

The lawyer explained each stage of the proceedings which began with signing the *compromis de vente*. This quite literally means 'the compromise of sale' – the agreement between the parties of what is to be purchased for what price. The contract is a standard one where the only get out clauses (*conditions suspensives*) related to us obtaining a suitable mortgage. Other *conditions suspensives* which could have applied, related to planning reports and the owner's authority to sell.

So, in this case, as we were paying cash, we were in fact already committed. If we backed out we lost our ten per cent deposit. The positive side of this is that there is no French word that translates as guzumping.

The document also set out the responsibilities of the vendor and purchaser, and indicated our responsibilities in maintaining fencing and rights of access. The section of stream that passed under the ancient packhorse bridge and ran alongside the property was jointly owned with our neighbour. I was asked to imagine drawing a notional line down the middle. Our fishing and navigation rights ended at that invisible line. Although, in theory, there was nothing to prevent me luring a trout away from my neighbour's bank by dangling a tasty maggot in my half of the stream, navigation was more complex. As the stream was just two and a half metres wide the lawyer suggested that I could perhaps negotiate an informal flexible agreement of mutual rights to cover such matters as course-plotting and mooring. It was also pointed out that as the stream had a name – L' Odorat – it was, strictly speaking, a river. This, however had no legal significance.

Property surveys, at least of the truncated kind we have become used to in the UK for valuation purposes, are not required in France. Indeed, even if you are arranging a French mortgage the lending organisation very rarely bothers to check the property. This is largely because the maximum possible loan is usually pegged at 80% of the purchase price.

However, there can be no doubt that a full survey (*géomètre*) is a good idea. The outcome is a document which describes the property in detail, lists all its faults and prioritises repairs. The survey can be used as a negotiating tool but only if you have not already signed the *compromis de vente*. The way round this would have been, with the vendor's agreement, to have added a suspensive survey clause to the *compromis de vente*. This could have said, for instance:

'*The purchaser need not proceed if the architect/surveyor reports that in his opinion works of repair costing, in his estimation, more than €50,000 are essential.*'

With the benefit of hindsight there can be no doubt that we should have opted for this. But survey charges were not included in *Les Maisons Formidable's* '*all inclusive fee*' and the full *géomètre* is expensive and the negotiations that inevitably follow can take time. With a property very obviously in need of TLC it is easy for the vendor to argue that all faults, however drastic, are already reflected in the price. It then comes down to whether you want to pull out of the deal or not and that remains an emotional decision, albeit an informed one.

So, in practice, it often comes down to how much you can trust your builder. Or, in our case how much we could trust the estate agent who recommended the builder. The important thing seemed to be that Kevin was registered. This meant that he was working legally and his qualifications and experience met the required trade standards in France. It was a kind of assurance.

We knew that local tradesman play 'spot the bodger'. They will happily shop him and will even do so with special relish if he is not French. Also it is worth noting that all exterior changes to property are checked to see if the work has been carried out properly. If something is wrong, and it is shown that you have used an unregistered builder, you could just end up in the same dock as the unhappy cowboy.

As well as this there is the tax angle. In theory all improvements can be taxed on a local basis and again when you come to sell the property. The local increase is unlikely to amount to much and even Capital Gains Tax is only usually a problem if you over develop; it is intended primarily to catch those who are, in effect, professional developers. To set against this charge is the 'original value of the property' (the purchase price) and an element of indexation if property values have increased. You can also claim back most of your costs which means keeping receipts and invoices which must, of course, come from registered suppliers and tradesmen.

One of the things that was most obviously wrong with the exterior of this property was that the shower emptied itself via a purpose-placed pipe down the wall below. From there, apart from a damp patch and a few puddles, the flow continued into the garden. The arrangement for waste water from the kitchen was similar, but according to Kevin, no surveyor would have bothered to comment on this. It was, certainly for its time, the standard design for grey water disposal. Standard it may be, but it was also worrying, and it could just be expensive to put right.

In France older properties are bought 'as seen' although the owner is obliged to reveal all known defects. But as La Maison D'Etre was, in effect, one massive defect this was not particularly helpful. However, it was agreed (ahead of us signing the contract) that Kevin would to be allowed access to poke around with a screwdriver to back up his assessment or to prove, at least, that the building would not imminently collapse in a heap of rubble. Well, at least that was the theory.

Through various searches and certificates the *acte authentique* clearly identified the property and its 'domains'. These documents also referred to the relevant planning regulations, easements and guarantees. In effect this confirmed everything set out in the *compromis de vente* as well as providing us with an analysis of the use of the property during the previous 50 years. La Maison D'Etre had in turn been the residence of a minor *comte*, a farm, a restaurant, a home for superannuated priests and a husky breeding farm. It was not so much a slippery slope as a cliff fall of decline.

The total cost of buying the property was something like £28,000. This was made up of the purchase price plus legal fees, stamp duty, land transfer, and regional and local taxes. Included in the total was £6,000 to *Les Maisons Formidable*. We now know that a French agent would have charged a fraction of that amount. It would have been cheaper still if we had bought directly through a *notaire* or had found the property in a local small ad. There had also been nothing in the legal labyrinth that had not been dealt with routinely by the *notaire*.

But *Les Maisons Formidable* did keep their promise of further assistance following the purchase. Just days after we took possession of the property a letter arrived. They hoped that the purchase of the property would bring us great joy. They also offered '*a continuing range of professional services and advice for just £100 an hour*'. Cheap at twice the price, no doubt.

Some aspects of their working practice were extremely cynical. The idea, for instance, of income from either a *gîte* or a bed and breakfast operation had been appealing; it could even have been crucial to our survival. They made it sound so easy by totally ignoring the practicalities of setting up any kind of business, which should have at least included considering the location and the costs of appropriate facilities and marketing. Of course, I should have known better.

Two years on, we are still waiting for someone from *Les Maisons Formidable* to '*pop round for a cup of tea*'. The pot is cold now. Doris has promised, however, should they call, to boil up a nice big kettle of very hot water.

More than half a million Brits own a second home abroad. But some banks, including some big high street names are still charging up to 4% over the odds for currency exchange. The difference between the best and the worst can be as much as £3,000 on a property costing £70,000.

One thing we got right was making the most of the exchange rate. We had bought euros forward, betting, in effect, against the pound. I'd watched the market trend for weeks before purchasing on line through www.fcukdirect.com. They are efficient and competitive; I have used them before and will do so again.

Even if you are doing an instant transfer, you should shop around. The specialist foreign currency houses should be top of your list. Your high street bank could just be competitive and you may even get a decent rate from Visa or, at a pinch, check out the Post Office. If convenience is more important than common sense buy at the port of entry, and if you really want to throw money away, any travel agent will be happy to oblige. The difference between the best and the worst deals on offer is considerable; in our case it paid for a nice set of kitchen units.

5
Moving In

La Maison D'Etre legally became our future home on August 2nd 2002. But it was almost a year later – when Doris retired in July 2003 – when we moved in. Well, 'moved in' is a slight exaggeration, the truth was the house was still 100% uninhabitable.

Kevin had laid down a gravel area to put the caravan on and had tapped into the house electrics so we could have a 'hook up'. He had also attached a hosepipe to the only tap in the house which provided a water supply at constant pressure.

'Well, we've always wanted our own caravan site,' said Doris.

Photo 4 Our own caravan site

We had hoped by now to have made at least some progress with the renovation. Kevin had promised that essential repairs – such as the barn roof – would already have been dealt with. However, it had proved impossible to cajole him from the other side of the Channel or during our flying visits to France.

'Sorry,' he said, 'I've been snowed under with work. But now you're here you will have my special attention. Don't worry, you'll be in by winter.'

We had arranged for our furnishings to be delivered. Temporarily they would have to be stored under tarpaulins in the barn. This was unsatisfactory, but cheaper than leaving them in store in the UK. When you add in insurance, storing a typical houseful of furniture with a remover costs at least £50 a week.

As you come down the hill on the way into the village from the north the first thing you see is a clump of trees, then, as the road narrows to the old pack horse bridge there is a sign announcing 'L'Odorat'. On crossing the river La Maison D'Etre is the first house. The village name plate is attached to the side of the house, the post box is embedded in the wall below a large mirror for the benefit of drivers approaching what amounts to the village's only crossroad. On the other side of the road a large lamp illuminates the junction with the light reflected from the mirror and the windows. At night this Christmas tree effect adds to the stature of the property. The longest-term residents are a colony of bats that feed on moths and, as yet, other unidentified flying insects, which are attracted by the lamp.

We plumbed in the washing machine as a matter of urgency. It died on the first rinse cycle. The machine had survived six previous moves so this demise was not totally unexpected, but my suspicions remain that a post mortem would have revealed dodgy French electrics, or at least a combination of French water and reduced voltage.

Photo 5 The new washing machine and the old electrics

I reminded Doris that the old village *lavabo* (washing place) was strategically placed just across the road so that the dirt discharged directly into the river. This I considered to be a silver lining. Doris's response was that not even her shortest-term plans included scrubbing my underwear in full view of the local population. That was fair enough. We began our search for a new machine immediately.

We sorted the pile of junk mail that had not yet been discarded; there were plenty of electrical goods on offer, but almost all were subject to monstrous delivery charges. Apart from FNAC, which trades only in the larger towns and cities, we couldn't really find an equivalent of Comet and Currys. Set against this, even modest-sized towns have the kind of specialist retailers which provide an excellent service. So we went to nearest decent-sized town – Ruffec – and found a specialist supplier.

The salesman demonstrated a masterpiece of Teutonic engineering that could not only adjust to various water types but had programmes to perform all laundry functions you can imagine and some you may prefer not to. This was the cleansing equivalent of a NASA probe: smart, cutting edge, and ludicrously expensive. We went for it.

But I baulked at the delivery charge: an extra €20 to shift the machine a few kilometres.

'If it is so clever,' I argued, 'why not just give it a couple of euro and tell it to come on the bus?'

Either my French wasn't up to it, or washing machine salesmen are born with the humour switch jammed in the off position. We paid up.

At least the shower in the house worked in the sense that it discharged water, and, as this was France in August, it was hugely welcome. During the first few days we both became skilled at bobbing and weaving around the cubicle to balance the hot steam and cold plunge effect. Later I found that if I turned the shower on and hid within the plastic wrap of the shower curtain, I could then leap out to enjoy a minute or so of safe ablutive rapture. Doris's technique was more scientific, she determined that the pulses from the showerhead were arpeggios of temperature and if you picked the right sequence of notes there was little to fear. I never quite worked this out.

We were prepared to put up with the shower, the rising damp, the leaky roof, the venerable gas-fired water heating system in the kitchen, the lack of adequate cooking facilities and even a proper bed to sleep in. Six months of living in a caravan had given us a siege mentality, and the cavalry – exemplified by Kevin's ample trouser cleavage – was coming to the rescue. He had promised that our problems would be sorted out *toute de suite*.

'Just as long as we are in for the winter,' I said.

It was amazing how many of the locals were taking an interest in what we were doing. It wasn't so much nosiness as civic pride: one tatty house makes those around it look tatty.

One very old man, *Monsieur* Crochet, would sometimes sit in the shade on the green opposite the house and monitor our progress. He could not see much, full stop, but he enjoyed the sounds and smells associated with building.

'Is the plastering going well, *Monsieur*?' He would ask.

'Very well,' I would say, 'how did you know?'

'The aroma, *Monsieur*. It reminds me of when I was a young man. I would walk with my lover in the fields, after the rain. You know, when the sun begins to dry the corn. It was most romantic.'

And on another occasion, 'Have you finished treating the timbers, *Monsieur*?'

'Not quite, but how did you know?'

'The aroma, *Monsieur*. When I was a boy I used to visit my aunt in Pornic. It was sometimes early in the year when they took all the small boats out of the water for repair. The smell of varnish always reminds me of the sea, *Monsieur*.'

On another occasion he asked me if we had successfully dealt with the problems of the septic tank. No, I didn't ask. Perhaps I should have done.

6
Beginning the Restoration

The main house remained a patchwork of small dark rooms with walls covered in resplendently vile wallpaper and a beigey-brown mould. The barn at the side was serviceable only as a storage and work area. The rest – apart from the shower and a rather fine example of a 19th century water closet in time-yellowed porcelain – was pretty much a no go area.

But Kevin's efforts began to make a difference; he cured the worst of the leaks by insulating the inside of the roof and, by removing walls and partitions, the downstairs was temporarily one large room, apart from the kitchen.

Photo 6 Doris at work in the barn

This remained untouched because it stood on top of a partially flooded cellar. In effect the existing kitchen floorboards were life rafts suspended over a subterranean lake. This was something that Kevin had missed in his evaluation.

The cellar would have to be fully drained, sealed, and filled with rubble. Kevin's 'ball park figure' for this extra work was £500. Ultimately the bill was nearer £2,000.

When the boards came up there was an air gap of a couple of feet above the water level that was a nature reserve for spiders.

The water meter, which was also in the cellar, had to be moved outside. Kevin phoned the water people.

'Good news,' he said, 'it will only cost you €200 to €300. But there is a slight snag. This is France and this is August. So nothing is going to happen in a hurry.'

He was right. The water board made promises, but nothing happened.

'You'll have to wait until after the middle of the month,' said Kevin, 'then some of them will be back from holiday. The total staff now will be a few workmen on standby for emergencies and someone fielding the phone calls.'

'But we are an emergency,' said Doris.

'But look at it from their point of view. The lake has been here for ages and nobody, as far as we know, has drowned yet. But after the 15th there will be the odd manager in the office; a few days after that the first batch of working lads, back from their hols, will be getting over their hangovers. Then you will get some action.'

Again he was right. We had already learned that attitudes to work in France are different from those in Britain. Things are changing certainly, but a Frenchman still sees a job for life as his birthright.

You don't have to work particularly hard or be particularly bright to get it and measured indolence is all that is required to keep it.

It sometimes seems as though 'the French working week' is almost an oxymoron. Banks, restaurants and shops are generally closed on Mondays. Tuesday is the day set aside for political activity, which mostly means striking or skiving. Wednesday is a day off school for most children, which means that at least one parent stays at home. Not much gets done on Friday, which is now regarded as part of *Le Weekend*. This leaves Thursday where there is a sudden urgent flurry of activity.

I was out on the particular Thursday when a young man came round to view our lake. Doris said he was very nice. Sympathetic. Understanding. His was also the owner of a sleek red soft-top car.

'This is my kitchen,' she said, gesturing at the water-filled gaping hole.

He read the situation immediately. I think Doris's cries of anguish may have helped. Anyway, two days later they arrived to do the job.

They were a couple of almost stereotypical French workmen – polite, hard working and easy to get on with. The problem was it was still August and they had not been able to get their hands on essential supplies – most specifically what was required in the way of washers.

'The warehouse she is still on holiday, *Madame*,' one of them explained.

'But can we get on with it anyway?' we pleaded.

Goodness knows when they would have come back if we'd let them go.

They said they would do their best but admitted that they had had

41

to improvise. If the washers were wrong, things could be a bit iffy. And sure enough, two days later the joint in the cellar started to leak.

'You'll have to go down and fix it,' Kevin said, looking at me.

'But I don't know how,' I protested.

'Well, OK,' he said, 'you get down there, tell me what's happening down there and I'll tell you what to do.'

I know it sounds crazy – as I was paying the bills – but that's how it was, my head in spiders' webs, water wobbling over my wellies and working its way up through the wick of my clothing. Can't beat being retired, I thought.

I worked like a diver under tuition and stopped the leak. Then Kevin had another bright idea.

'We could cut a hole through the cellar wall into the barn next door, so if the problem happens again you won't have to pull up your nice kitchen floor.'

He was right in the sense that the barn is attached to the house and is a couple of feet lower. The problem was the wall in-between: it was almost a metre thick.

Kevin had spotted a heavy duty hammer drill with high speed bits.

'Get that,' he said, 'at £17 it's a snip.'

Kevin, it had to be said, was good as spotting bargains, though I noticed he never paid for them himself.

Equipped with this new weapon I worked by the light of a suspended torch, again I was guided by his voice from above. If he got fed up with instructing me he would make life more interesting by playing a trick or two. His favourite was to wait until I was waist high in water with an electrical drill in my hand before turning off the power. Hilarious. Well, he found it so anyway.

It took several hours to break through to the barn. The drill went through the stone easily enough, the snag was that the bit was only about six inches long, so I also needed the use of a steel bar with a clump hammer. But I knew I was getting there even before I saw daylight: the cellar began to empty.

Little pieces of history began to appear from beneath the water line: there were beer crates, large lumps of charred wood and a pair of soaking but serviceable oars which I resolved to varnish and find a suitable place to display. They make an interesting talking point.

The cellar also contained enough paper, packaging and soaking rag to fill a small skip; clearing it out was not a pleasant job.

I had been told that Germans had been billeted in the house during the war and as they left they set fire to it, either on purpose, or accidentally. Those in the 'deliberate fire' camp hinted at some sort of retribution, possibly linked to a scandal, while those who believed the fire was accidental talked about a log falling from the kitchen grate. We would probably never know, but there was evidence enough of the fire itself in charred roof timbers and those that appeared as the water drained away.

Upstairs we had decided to remodel the space to create three bedrooms (one *en suite*), an open office area and a bathroom. Because of the size of the house we could create for ourselves the size and scale of bedroom in which Marie Antoinette's dresses could be easily accommodated, but this meant that we had to be less generous elsewhere and the other bedrooms would be more modest.

We pushed on with partitioning work. Hollow clay blocks – which have excellent damp and sound proof qualities – were simply too heavy for upstairs. Gypsum fibre, which also has admirable damp resistance properties, is excellent for lining walls but can be a touch pricey, so we went for plasterboard which is both inexpensive and easy to use while being relatively light – which is perfect for upstairs and ideal for non-load bearing walls.

Until recently, plasterboard was most commonly mounted on a timber frame which was often used as a feature itself but we opted for light metal which helps keep the panels flat and rigid. The other benefit is that it is easy to slide insulation material – such as rockwool – between two panels. A similar system of waterproof panels (*plâques hydrofugées*) was to be used for the separate bathroom and *en suite*.

Photo 7 The master bedroom in preparation

The plan now was to fill the cellar with hardcore – around 30 tonnes of it. Kevin had already bought the hardcore which was stored at the local farm. In the meanwhile we threw into the cellar every stone we came across.

As we waited for the cellar to dry we fitted a back degreaser. Like most rural properties in France, we are on septic drainage which means that everything from the toilet is channelled into a *fosse septique* – a large tank fitted with overflow pipes that filter the excess underground. Everything else in the tank is dealt with organically, but it is surprisingly easy to kill off the fermentation bugs – one person in the home taking antibiotics can do it. To make sure the system remains efficient every three months we put in a commercial product called *Eparcyl* (*Septifosis* is a popular alternative). These products contain microbes that feast off the solids and are a massive improvement on the traditional method of activating bacteria which featured a deceased and well rotted rat.

The back degreaser takes away grey water – that is any used water that does not go down the loo, it separates grease by floating it to the surface. The tank itself – a second large concrete container with a minimum capacity of 200 litres – is buried in the ground, again with pipes which drain the excess water. This goes into a bed of gravel for filtering and the rest finds its way via a pipe system to the *fosse septique* to join in the fermentation process. Well, at least that is what is supposed to happen.

It is tricky to check just how well an old *fosse* is working because it is buried underground. Complete excavation is horrendously expensive and a *Time Team* type dig may not pin-point smaller leaks. There are inspection covers but even an expert can miss something, and it is often the fitting of degreasers that causes the problem because old septic tanks – fitted a generation or more ago – are simply too small to treat all the extra waste flowing from showers and sinks, washing machines and dishwashers. In the past this was allowed to drain away into the ground but as this is no longer acceptable, degreasers have become *de rigeur*. But systems that are inefficient or overloaded have become ecological time bombs. Eventually someone will impose monitoring – there could soon be a Septic Police.

Some very specific regulations are already in place: extractor vents must be positioned at the exit end of the tank which itself must be placed more than 20 centimetres underground, 35 metres from a well or watercourse, and a minimum of five metres from the property it serves.

The hole we needed for the degreaser was a big one. Kevin hired us a *tracteur pelle* for two days – this is basically a JCB with a digger. Kevin had a great time using this. Two of his daughters came along to watch him and it was great to see the swelling pride in their eyes as he swung the bucket about. We for our part flinched a bit when he hit our caravan with it! It was still our home, but the damage wasn't serious.

Perhaps I should have seen the lake under the kitchen floor as a warning of where we were going wrong. At least symbolically.

I could perhaps put down the fact that I was paying the workman and doing most of the work myself as a significant, if sometimes soggy learning curve, but the problem went deeper. Kevin's guesstimates and ball park figures always seemed to be as optimistic as joining the Dutch Mountain Rescue.

But we were novices and he knew it. We were not expert at DIY and had little knowledge of French building regulations – particularly with regard to electrics. Worse still, although our conversational French was adequate, we did not have enough of the specialist builder's vocabulary or an understanding of the subtler nuances and differences in the materials used in French buildings.

Working on the principle that a little knowledge is generally more dangerous than none, we had long determined that we would put ourselves in Kevin's dinner-plate sized hands. Indeed, finding him still seemed to be an extraordinary stroke of luck. Apart from anything else language problems were limited to Yorkshire talking to Black Country. Bad enough but not insurmountable.

There are two main ways of paying a builder: the first way is to agree a daily rate and buy or pay for the materials yourself. The rate is around €100 a day. We later learned that most French builders also prefer to work this way because they are on the 'Micro Enterprise' scheme which significantly cuts their tax bill if they can earn less than €29,000 a year. Buying materials themselves clouds the issue. It is surprising how the income of many 'small' builders remains just below the (annually adjusted) threshold. The second way to pay is to get a *devi* which is broadly similar to an estimate in England. Because there was so much work to do we started off with an initial large *devi* from Kevin.

Kevin's *devis* looked so reasonable that I immediately commissioned what had now become high priority extra work. This included having the cellar filled in. It was only Doris's note of caution that prevented me from letting the list of new work and 'ball park' figures get out of hand.

'I think we should see how it goes,' she said.

And she was proved right. Particularly as it all went horribly wrong.

I should perhaps have seen it coming but there is no fool like an old fool. However, it is impossible to anticipate everything that will need doing when you renovate a property and, if that property is in France, the problem is compounded by kinds of infestation and rot that are unknown on British shores.

Typically, what happened was this: Kevin would be about to deliver the *coup de grâce* to a wall you had asked him to remove when he points out a rotten joist. What you should do is say 'Hey, I can see that this is going to be a whole new job, so go home and write me out a new *devis*.' But you don't, you say, 'OK, let's replace the joist.' And in the process of doing that you find that three other joists have been termite breakfast. Again you should say, 'Hey, we'll wait until they've had their lunch and then we'll put in a set of treated timbers,' but what you do is to pick up the yellow pages and start ringing round the timber yards. And so, on it went. A little extra expense here. A little more effort there. What was worse was that we were beginning to hear horror stories of renovation projects that had got so far out of hand that the owners had been forced to give up and sell. It was becoming clear how this could happen.

The time had come to take stock of the situation.

We came up with a mixed strategy: first we would re-prioritise. There was no hurry, for instance, to do anything with the barn, equally we could leave a lot of the external restoration. The pointing was tatty in places but, as the building had stood for centuries, it could surely wait a bit longer.

Photo 8 David at work in the barn

As far as the interior was concerned, we would just have to say no to anything that was not absolutely necessary. Equally, we would have to do rather more for ourselves. But there were still some important aspects of the renovation that could not be done without expert help. We still had two main rooms downstairs, for instance, and wanted one large one. We therefore asked Kevin if we could take down the dividing wall.

'That's no problem,' he said 'it's not load bearing.'

And with this assurance we said 'go ahead please'.

He removed the dividing wall and reinforced the ceiling above with substantial pine beams supported by pine uprights. We were surprised only that he had used pine because hard woods – oak for instance – are relatively cheap in France.

However, within a few days it was clear that the beam in the middle was sagging and twisting. This could be seen clearly from beneath it and from both sides – when crossing the landing we walked down a small hill and then back up again. What was even worse was that between the walls of the bedrooms and the floor there was now a gap big enough to push your fingers through.

If there was a moment when we could have thrown in the towel, it was now. But we could not afford to live in England, it would be near impossible to sell a property with such a glaring defect, and we also had the children to think of.

'We'll have to tackle Kevin,' Doris said, 'but it won't be easy. He does not like admitting mistakes.'

So it was decided to attack him with stealth. We had taken a lot of photographs before we moved in and had continued to do so as the work progressed. These pictures had been intended as no more than a personal record to help us remember events in our dotage.

Kevin claimed that the floor had always been dropping away but we had the pictures to prove that this was not true. He eventually conceded the point and ordered a replacement steel girder. A few days later he turned up with one girder and three large lads. We hid, mainly in the kitchen, whilst the operation was carried out. It was not only a success but was boxed in so neatly that we scarcely knew it was there.

Perhaps we should have said that this was a builder error too far. Kevin had only recently drilled holes for a toilet exit pipe four centimetres too high which meant I then had to shape a wooden pedestal to bring the toilet up to the level. We've lived with it ever since, but still think it looks bad. But we were so relieved that our ceiling was safe we backed off. Even the best builders make the occasional mistakes, don't they?

On days when Kevin did not turn up – and to our minds this was happening far too regularly – we had already begun to tackle some jobs we would not previously have considered taking on. It was also part of our new cost-cutting strategy, but even the apparently simple job can turn into a nightmare.

There was a dado rail about a metre long in our living room. It was spectacularly ugly. One morning Doris suggested that we remove it.

'No problem,' I said.

And it really was no problem. Two tweaks of the claw hammer and out it came. But the rail was rotten and the plaster underneath was blown; damp had got under it and lifted it away from the wall.

'I'm not sure about tackling this,' I said.

'Just take it back as far as you have to,' Doris suggested.

Photo 9 Doris with guests in the unrestored living room

So it was back to the claw hammer. With only the slightest encouragement a large rotten cupboard decomposed before our eyes exposing another area of blown plaster, then this came away equally easily revealing the bare stonework of the original recess. This, in turn, made the whole wall appear unbalanced because of a second matching cupboard. Back to the claw hammer. Same result.

There were now two gaping holes in the wall which at least created a measure of symmetry. Closer inspection confirmed that we had found the tip of the iceberg, pretty much all the plaster on the wall was blown, and the same applied to the window recess. We would have to strip back to the bare bones and replaster the lot. An hour later the room looked marginally worse than a bomb crater.

When the doorbell rang we swam in different directions through the debris to answer it and arrived at precisely the same moment. We must have looked like flour graders at the end of a long shift.

7
A History Lesson

Our visitor was a French female, as time worn as our roofing joists, and sporting an unseasonable black shawl.

'Monsieur, Madame, je m'appelle Madame Toutanu.'

The name had a resonance. We had heard of Celestine Toutanu, formerly owner of the property. She had apparently left the village as a young woman to follow (the then) dubious career of actress which had been at least a modest success. When she returned, in the final flush of youth, with a husband who (it was said) had been her 'manager', she took over the house, which had been left to her in her father's will, and turned it into a restaurant. The walls had sported framed posters featuring herself in various productions of French farces. She called the restaurant 'L'Hibou Qui Péte'.

To her husband, *Monsieur* Basil Toutanu, she was more Sybil than Celestine. It was said that her tongue could strip wallpaper and it was he who was the most regular recipient of her venom. And he had to suffer it – she was the proprietor. After almost 20 years of this cruel and unnatural punishment, he left her to run away with a diminutive but perfectly proportioned waitress. It had been the greatest scandal in the village since the First World War when the four score and something *Monseigneur* Lefebre and his 20-year-old housekeeper had both succumbed to toxic fumes in the same double bed.

Celestine Toutanu soon gave up the unequal task of running the restaurant alone and moved first into a small house the village, then into a tiny sixth floor apartment in a nearby town. She told us this with such a snarl of resentment that we imagined we were partly responsible for her misfortune. Doris rescued the situation by producing our 'finds' from the barn. There were several bottles of wine which tasted like battery acid, as well as a couple of bottles of *Cognac* which we intended to keep for a special occasion. There was also a bottle of *absinthe*. We offered her *Cognac* or *absinthe*. She took the *absinthe*.

'*C'est très profitable,*' she assured us, '*pour la gorge.*'

The anticipation of soothing her throat mellowed her mood and she began to tell us, in hesitant but determined English, some of the history of the property. Since her departure it had been occupied, off and on, for rather less than four years. The most recent owners, the husky breeders, had moved to Canada – presumably as there would be a bigger market for their dogs.

She told us that the property had originally been a farmhouse. During the Second World War, it had been used for billeting Germans who apparently did not like it very much and as they left, they set fire to it. The fire had surged straight upwards through the roof taking away around half of it before the *Sapeurs Pompiers* brought the blaze under control. The damaged sections were rebuilt with new timbers which were then covered in traditional slate tiles. The expense, which must have been considerable, was apparently borne by a remorseful German military. But this was 'Free France' – too much resentment made it unpoliceable. The new timbers and expensive tiles were little enough to pay for an easy life.

'Today, if you talk with the old men you will hear that all of them, with their brothers, fathers and uncles, were war heroes – fighters in *La Resistance*. Also, you will hear that there was no man in

Entrechoux who was a friend to the Germans, or a collaborator. Little of this is true, *Monsieur*. It is, as you say in England, a lot of shoemakers.'

'A load of cobblers?'

'*Certainement Monsieur*, cobblers. There was *un peu de resistance* and there was *un peu de collaboration*. But for most people it was *rien* – nothing. *Ils ont continue avec leur existence fastidieuse.*'

'Their boring lives?'

'Tedious I think is better, *Monsieur*. Tedious. They imagine the war does not happen here. This is not only Entrechoux, *Monsieur*, it was every village in the Charente. It is, I think, *la nature humaine.*'

'Human nature?'

'That also, *Monsieur*. One day I will tell you what really happen. I will tell you *la verité*. The truth, *Monsieur*, the truth. *C'est une histoire sensationelle.* You will make wet in your trousers.'

'I'll wet myself?'

'Only if you drink too much *absinthe, Monsieur*. I hope you will not.'

Celestine took a sip of her drink and giggled. Then, after composing herself with several deep breaths, she continued.

'Today I instruct you how your house became 'Le Petit Chateau'. It is, *naturellement*, first the size of your erection, *Monsieur*. *C'est certainement la plus grande du village*. It is also the new slate roof which the Germans pay for. It is *traditionelle, Monsieur*. All *chateaux* have the grey tiled roof. *C'est bien distingué.*'

'Distinguished?'

'Yes, *Monsieur*, and *distinctif* also.'

The property's nickname – 'Le Petit Chateau' – had certainly stuck despite the temporary transformation after the war into 'L'Hibou Qui Péte'. This other name, explained Celestine, was a French pun. Just as the most common French name for a hotel is 'Le Lion D'Or' – either 'The Golden Lion' or 'Bed and Sleep' according to your take – 'L'Hibou Qui Péte' was 'The Farting Owl' or 'Ibo Capet'. Celestine, now sipping her third class of *absinthe*, explained:

'When the Germans come to the Charente we were not permitted to celebrate Jeanne D'Arc. She was *dangereaux*. A maker of trouble. A fighter of freedom. So now we shout the name 'Ibo Capet' whose sons make the beginning of the state of France. Ibo Capet is to France as *Monsieur* Jean Bull is to *Angleterre*. But the Germans did not know this. All they cared about was *Cognac* and sex. Especially sex.'

'But what about the farting owl?' I asked.

Celestine's face had become flushed. She cast the shawl aside as she refilled her glass. Her English, although regularly derailed, was now bold, and her voice was strident.

'When I was a girl,' she said, 'if someone accidentally break the wind at dinner we would say there was an owl up the chimney. The sound you see, was an echo of the voice of the bird.'

Celestine demonstrated this implausibility by wrapping her swollen knuckles together and blowing through the gap between her thumbs. The sound produced was perfectly pitched between fart and hoot. With measured *gravitas* she repeated this three times.

'There you have it, *Monsieur*. *C'est un rendement magnifique, non?*'

As she turned to pick up her glass we applauded. She filled the glass again in recognition of our acclaim.

'Perhaps, *Monsieur* and *Madame*, one day I will show you *ma pièce especial*. It is of a young curé at the confessional after eating too much garlic and *foie gras*.'

'Perhaps you will, *Madame*,' I said, 'no doubt it will be a *tour de force*.'

She downed her glass and rose a little unsteadily. I moved to assist her and held her arm as we moved to the door. She turned, smiled, and then insisted on kissing us both goodbye.

'Thank you for your hospitality, *Monsieur*, *Madame*. The drink has made me, how do you say, a little sentimental.'

'We have a saying in England,' I told her, '*absinthe* makes the heart grow fonder.'

'Really, *Monsieur*?'

'No, not really, it's a joke, a play on words, like *l'hibou qui péte*.'

'Perhaps you will explain when I visit again. I may visit again?'

'*Certainement*, *Madame*, you are always welcome.'

She smiled and began to shuffle down the street. Then, almost as an afterthought, she turned and waved both hands at us.

'Then I bid you *au revoir*,' she said.

After Celestine left we both had visions of impromptu performances, for the entertainment of diners, whilst her husband cowered in the darkest corners of the dining room. She remained a legend in the village. We came to use her as a barometer of taste; we mentioned the name and waited for a response. Some smiled. Some shook their heads. When I went to the *Mairie* with my carefully drawn plans for larger windows, I was already known as the latest in the line of subsequent owners who had entertained Celestine Toutanu.

Monsieur Cabacou, the Mayor, stared solemnly over the upper rim of his reading glasses.

'I regret,' he said, 'that Celestine is, as we say *Monsieur*, *une femme de chagrin*. It is rumoured that she has some terrible secret. But I cannot say if that is so. But she is a woman I believe who was once both ambitious and beautiful. That is a dangerous recipe *Monsieur*.'

8
Plaster and Politics

Oddly enough 'a dangerous recipe' was pretty much what Kevin called the plaster mix we made for the living room walls. It was basically what we would call Plaster of Paris, too heavy a mix and it dries like chalk, too light and it slides from the surface like snow from a shovel.

Kevin had demonstrated the mix method; not too much at a time, a clean bucket and scoop – I used a 500 gram plastic honey pot. Then it's one scoop of water and two scoops of plaster plus a scoop of something called *Presylis 35* which decelerates setting. It is almost impossible to mix by hand: I used an electric drill with an attachment that worked like a food mixer. Finally I tested the mixture and added more water, a drop at a time, until I had a thick porridge.

This basic plaster mix – or *plâtre* – dries so quickly you have to work like an anabolically enhanced window cleaner. You start at the bottom and work up, floating the mix smoothly upwards and outwards; it dries almost as you go. Experts can handle a mix of four to one with two scoops of water. I had bought the basic plastering tools which included a filler knife and a metal float but they rusted instantly so I binned them and bought a new set in stainless steel.

The amazing thing about the French method is the coverage, the exposed wall was built of large irregular stones about eighteen inches thick and some of the gaps were six to eight inches. In England you fill the gaps with mortar and render it before plastering over but in France you pack in plaster with a filling knife. Even the deeper recesses were touch dry by the time I had made the mix for the top coat. A light sanding produced a surface that was ready for decorating the following day.

It was around this time that I made another visit to the *Mairie*. I was already becoming aware of just how important and powerful the Mayor is in France. For example, Kevin had told us that his daughter had signed up for a school trip to Spain and that, as part of the protocol, she had to be given written permission from the *Mairie* to be absent from the commune. This has at least something to do with local accountability, but perhaps not in the sense it would be understood in Britain. In rural communities a child may be absent from school for several days – say for harvesting. This is considered reasonable. But what would happen, for instance, if harvesting coincided with some other activity – like a school trip perhaps – which would be otherwise beyond the control of the commune? There could be misunderstanding, even conflict. To avoid this a note is required.

Kevin had assured us that we did not need planning permission for internal changes. But anything outside – or anything that could be seen from outside – was different, and that included matters that may be considered largely cosmetic. We wanted to pull down a wall constructed from crumbling brick and replace it with breeze blocks.

'You take a picture of the wall as it is,' said Kevin, 'then draw a sketch of the alterations you want to make. Then you go to the Mayor, on your knees, and ask nicely.'

The Entrechoux *Mairie* is a small stone-fronted, ground-floor office situated between the redundant *pissoir* and the former fire station. Occasionally, as on my previous visit, *Monsieur* Cabacou, *Le Maire* himself, is in attendance, but when he has other business – such as delivering the post – the office is most regularly staffed by Madelaine, the wife of a motorcycle mechanic who travels noisily each day to work in Ruffec.

Madelaine has a winning smile and a big bundle of patience. What we could not manage in French was accomplished in sign language and when she was sure she had the thrust of each point she made notes which were later attached to the photograph and sketch. She explained that all this was necessary to obtain the *'Declaration de Permis de Constuire'* and a copy would be sent to the local tax office. I was a touch concerned about this, but Madelaine explained that it would make no difference to my tax bill, a swimming pool perhaps, but not a replacement wall. The documents had to be sent in anyway. As soon as I had my permission I had two years to complete the work, otherwise the process would have to begin again.

'You will know in two weeks,' she said, 'but there will be no problem.'

'How do you know?' I asked.

'Because you have done it properly,' she said. 'The papers must be correct. That is all. Otherwise they come back.'

'I will remember that,' I said.

'And I will assist you *Monsieur*.'

'Thank you,' I said.

'There are some people,' she said looking towards the window, 'who do not care to be correct. Their paper comes back many times. Many times.'

I knew she was speaking of what the villagers called the 'Ghetto'. This was where nine English families were all packed into a *cul de sac* of modern housing.

'I apologise for the extra work caused by some of the English,' I said.

'It is not because they are English, *Monsieur*, it is because they are ignorant. No charm, no manners, no sense. We call them *"Les dindons"*.'

'The turkeys?'

'Because they run round in circles and have no sense. But they make a lot of noise.'

'I am not *un dindon?*'

'No *Monsieur*, you are *un pigeon*. You fly around. You look. You see. You eat. It is a compliment *Monsieur*.'

'Thank you,' I said.

And that, as it turned out, was the seminal lesson in French bureaucracy. Get help. Get it right. Get whatever you want. Nobody cares very much what it is. But it helps if you are a pigeon.

9
Etiquette and the Septic Tank

We were beginning to learn some of the essential differences between France and the UK: any time that you meet someone in France, friend or tax collector, you shake hands.

We were babysitting some cats. I had gone to feed them at our friend's house when a huge man appeared. He was a farmer neighbour, who owned the mill. He approached me in an aggressive manner and was obviously upset about something. The first thing that he did was to put out his hand to shake. He then complained furiously about water that was flooding his meadow. I was able to assure him that it was not our friend's fault.

If the person you are meeting has been doing manual or dirty work they will offer their wrist or even their finger to shake. The only exception to the etiquette of the handshake, that I know of, is the *fosse* emptying man. He keeps his hands behind his back and inclines his head in a curt bow of acknowledgement.

I have been told that in recent memory, when the *fosse* needed emptying the local farmer would come along, remove the contents and spread them on his land. This was recycling at its best and most basic. Ultimately you could buy the farmer's produce, eat it, and – a day of two later – begin the process again.

But this is no longer legal. You have to call out a specialised firm who come along, do the same job as the farmer used to, and charge twice as much. That's progress.

As there was also no possible DIY option we telephoned a specialist and the next day along came a man in a truck with a large tank and a pipe. The principle is pretty much the reverse of filling your gas tank. The main difference being that whilst propane is odourless, methane is not. Tanks are installed to match the 'output' of the property according to its size. Ours was large capacity – around 3,000 litres.

We had discovered that large septic tanks are a status symbol – rather like Range Rovers in Surrey that are suburbanly scrubbed on Saturday mornings before the weekly expedition to the outback of Sainsbury's.

'*Trois milles litres, Monsieur, c'est exceptionelle. Je pense, peut-être que vous avez la plus grande fosse…*'

But the size of your tank is not a licence to lord it over those who are not similarly endowed, as that would be bad form.

'*C'est necessaire, Monsieur, c'est necessaire,*' you say.

As the cost of the pump-out is partly determined by the amount of effluent pumped, the first task is to check that the *fosse* is full which is achieved by lifting the concrete lid and peering into the abyss below. I was prepared to take it as read that our cup floweth over, but the pump-out man insisted that I peered alongside him. His Gallic shrug and scratch of the head indicated that the *fosse* had almost reached the point where neighbourhood evacuation notices would have to be posted.

'*C'est tout plein, Monsieur.*'

'*Mais oui, c'est tout plein,*' I agreed without hesitation.

He left the tank lid on the ground and returned to the truck for the clipboard with the necessary triplicate paperwork. I signed the forms and was about to retreat when he began to talk football. He asked me who the best footballer in England was.

I told him that I didn't really have an opinion. In fact my only rational opinion, at this stage, was that the man had absolutely no sense of smell – perhaps a necessary qualification for his occupation.

Again he insisted I deliver a name for discussion.

'Michael Owen,' I ventured.

He nodded twice as if he had just encountered an eternal and undeniable truth. He smiled slowly, sucked his teeth, and then responded in impeccable English.

'Then it is not surprising,' he said, 'that the English football team stinks almost as much as your *fosse, Monsieur.*'

10
Gardens and Shutters

As the summer wore on the grounds of the house within the husky fence turned into a jungle of weeds and poppies. The Flymo and strimmer which we had imported from England had been sold as 'suitable for a medium-sized garden'. Here it was as useless as attacking a tank column with a water pistol.

Photo 10 The husky fence

Part of the problem is the cross Channel definition of 'medium sized'. The 1,000 or so square metres of land surrounding La Maison

D'Etre is enough for a modest housing estate in Kent, with every property having a 'medium-sized garden'. Come to think of it, the way developers now work in some parts of the UK there would probably be just enough land left over for a chidren's play park and a drive-through McDonald's. Interior space is considered adequate in Britain as long as there is room to squeeze in a 42 inch flat screen TV, while outside space is a waste of space.

In France 1,000 square metres is around average for a family home. It is certainly a medium-sized garden. Large gardens, and there are plenty of those, should be defined as 'requiring the services of a full time gardener'.

Photo 11 Doris relaxing in the garden

When you see vegetation take over so quickly it is quite a shock – you realise the enormity of what you have taken on. Although there are two short respites – in mid summer and mid winter – at other times everything grows at beanstalk rate in the Charente.

We know people who have bought a two hectare field for £250. Another friend who purchased a Charente property found that he had also acquired a field which he felt should be put to some good use so he let it to a farmer who grew pumpkins. We also know people who, almost as a footnote to the property sale, found that they had 'won' three extra small plots of land.

Even with planning permission for a decent-sized house you can still buy 1,000 square metre plots for £7,000, though you may choose to pay twice or even three times as much for a prime location. Indeed, one of the most cost effective ways of acquiring property in France is to buy a plot and have a *modèle* built on it. A *modèle* is basically a home chosen from a catalogue of designs which meet planning and building regulations. The build cost, excluding the fencing, is normally included in the price. A three bedroom *pavillon* may cost around £75,000. Even with fencing and legal costs it is therefore still possible to have a brand new family home for less than £120,000. Add to this the advantage of stage payments and tax breaks for new property and the equation can be irresistible, if you have the cash.

Kevin recognised our garden problem and offered to lend us a mower. Actually it wasn't so much a mower as an industrial strength pulverizer.

'I got it from a friend who got it from the council,' he said.

It was huge and red in colour so we christened it 'the Ferrari'. It handled with attitude – taking a wide line into corners before accelerating hard back into the straight. When you started it up it was seriously loud, then the revs built gradually to sonic boom.

We have since bought a new mower which cost a touch over £400 but it's the right kit for the job. It's a Honda and as bright and yellow as Noddy's car. I tell people I'm testing the engine, which is reassuringly quiet, for Eddie Jordan's F 1 team. Nobody seems to believe me. It now takes me about two and a half hours to cut the grass. The Ferrari did it in 20 minutes, but I still have all my toes and partial hearing.

The new strimmer cost £250 but at least it doesn't throw in the towel at the first sight of a weed. The big investment, however, is in time. During the peak growing season we reckon basic gardening duties take up two full working days each week. Oddly enough the estate agents didn't mention this commitment when they sold us a property with 'a medium-sized garden'.

The impression I have given is that we have a large lawn. It would perhaps be more accurate to say that we have a huge area of greenish fast-growing vegetation and one small area close to the house, which I had turfed. In this area garden chairs no longer leaned like old men on the way home from sampling the latest vintage. And, in the absence of chairs, it provided a soft landing area for children at play.

It was, of course, the only area in the garden that attracted a mole.

Fortunately the French have invented a cunning device to deal with the problem. It comprises a small cylinder which contains batteries and two wires, which connect to a little red packet. This is the explosive charge.

All you have to do is open the mole run, drop in the cylinder, and change the setting button from *securité* to *arme*, and throw a little earth over the top. Then you take a comfy seat, open a can of 1664, and wait.

The theory is that the mole finds the obstacle in the run and tries to dig it out of the way. The vibration triggers the charge and the mole emerges from the hole like the pieces of a jigsaw puzzle.

The only slight snag is this. It doesn't work. It is actually less successful *pro rata* than trying to seduce the creature to the surface by singing in moleish.

Over a fortnight of waiting I downed the best part of two cases of beer. It seemed to me by then that the options were either traditional mole traps or alcoholism. On the last evening of my vigil, in desperation I think, I cursed the mole in both slurred French and drunken English.

That did the trick. I have not seen a mole in the garden since.

Until you have lived in France it is difficult to believe just how wonderful shutters are. They keep a room cool through the summer heat and keep out the worst of the winter blasts. They also supply extra privacy and security. Old houses and creaky shutters go together, most commonly they droop on their hinges until they encounter the window ledge and will neither open nor close properly. If you are viewing an old house and find a heavy bolt and the shutters shut, be very suspicious.

Buying new shutters, especially if they are not a 'standard size', is expensive. We were quoted €330 a pair for the larger windows and this was in treated pine. One alternative was to take them apart, slat by slat, replacing rotten sections and tidying up the tongue and groove before reassembling, refitting and repainting.

Our shutters needed attention: the paintwork was tatty but the sag not significant. We considered the popular remedy of an iron reinforcement across the width of each panel and a lick of paint over the lot, but this could be storing up problems. Having scraped away a couple of investigative sections, a simple biopsy – performed by a surgical screwdriver – and discovered that the wood was worn but worthy, we stripped off the old paint, treated the timber and repainted. Simple as that. Well almost.

We first considered marine paint – the popular choice for properties near the sea – but as we are at least 130 kilometres from the coast, we decided that the windborne salt factor would be insignificant. A more serious option was micro-porous paint which allows the wood to breathe. In the end the matter was decided by history; our shutters had to be a fairly neutral grey – the only colour permitted within 500 metres of a listed ancient monument (the church) – and the matching options at *Monsieur Bricolage* were expensive and unsatisfactory. Paints from England are generally cheaper and of better quality, so this was pushed to the top of the shopping list for our impending short trip to Blighty.

11
A Load of Old Codgers

There is an annual event sponsored and organised by the local commune. It is the *Repas des Aines* – the old codgers' lunch. For us this is where the process of integration really began.

As I was of retirement age I got an invitation which was also generously extended to my '*parents*'. As the average age of those attending would be perhaps 70, I did not anticipate that many parents would attend – although they would, of course, be most welcome. The truth is that '*parent*' has a wider definition in France: it means 'relative'.

Well, the commune certainly knew how to look after us old codgers. The idea is to give us enough food at one sitting to keep us going all winter.

We began with *aperitifs* and *petits fours*, then it was traditional *potage* – vegetable soup – with Bordeaux wine. We were sitting close to old Maurice, the doyen of the hunt, who demonstrated how to keep the wine flowing. Whenever a bottle was empty, he picked it up, tapped it loudly with his spoon, and another one appeared. Not even Paul Daniels can do that.

I think we were on bottle four or five when the *vol-au-vents* arrived and I had lost count by the time we tucked into *Langue de boeuf à la Reine sauce piquante* (Cow's tongue in a spicy sauce). I was now feeling full and rosy cheeked. But this was not a repast for the faint-hearted. The next course was local lamb with haricot beans which was followed by cheese with lettuce and dressing. Finally, the main part of the meal was rounded off with strawberry *gâteau* and a sweet white wine. I tried to identify the wine by reading the label but found the lettering was out of focus.

Four hours after the meal had begun we were served coffee and liquors and by then I had the confidence to rattle along in French. Nobody seemed to mind the odd linguistic slip. They patted me on the back and smiled.

I knew that wild boar remained in pockets of forest and I had also read somewhere that there had been sightings of bear in France's mountainous fringes. I asked old Maurice about this.

Maurice is an octogenarian and, although his six foot frame is rather hunched, he is as lithe as many men 30 years younger. For at least 50 years he has maintained his reputation as a premier huntsman and spirited joker.

He shrugged his huge shoulders and filled his glass. Then he boomed aloud.

'*Monsieur* Johnson wants to know if we have bears here in Charente.'

'*Oui certainement Monsieur*,' said one voice.

'But not so many today,' said another.

'But you still have them?' I asked.

'*Mais oui, Monsieur*,' said another man, 'but they are, as we say, *protégé*.'

'Protected species,' I said helpfully.

'*Absolument Monsieur*.'

'And have any of you seen a bear? I mean recently.'

'*Certainement Monsieur*,' said Maurice, 'young François here escaped an attack only last week. Is this not true?'

Another grizzled hunting veteran rose unsteadily to his feet at the other end of the table. He was fully sixty years of age and flushed with wine. The epithet 'young', I was later to learn, was used to distinguish him from his father and grandfather who shared the same Christian name.

He hesitated for a moment and began:

'I was on the small hill beyond the ford. I was watching a buzzard making her nest. And then, there he was – standing no further from me than you are, *Monsieur*.'

He became silent. Everyone looked at me. I knew I was expected to contribute.

'And how did you escape?' I asked.

He had anticipated this.

'I dare not climb a tree, *Monsieur*, for the bear he can climb better than me. I ran, *Monsieur*. I ran like the rabbit from the fox. Down the hill.'

All those around me were nodding their heads. There was special import in 'down'.

'Down the hill?' I asked.

There were smiles around the room now. Knowing, I thought.

'*Monsieur*,' he said, 'I can tell you do not truly know the *chasse*. The bear is big and strong but he is not well balanced.'

'Balanced?'

'Yes, the legs at the back are powerful. Like Mercedes Benz he drives from the rear. He is very fast up the hill.'

'And down?'

'He is a clown, *Monsieur*. His front legs are short and not so strong. When he runs down the hill he falls. Sometimes he will turn over altogether. Arse over head. It is not elegant, *Monsieur*.'

I was trying to picture this. I could not do so other than in cartoon images.

'And so you see, *Monsieur*,' François concluded, 'if you meet a bear, do not climb a tree and do not run up the hill.'

'Run down, like the rabbit from the fox,' I said.

'That is correct, *Monsieur*.'

'Thank you,' I said.

François took his seat and began to fill his glass. There was silence for some moments. Then one or two people began to giggle. Finally there was a torrent of laughter.

12
The Log Burner

In the large room downstairs I had bricked up the fireplace with breeze blocks and rendered it, but as we were about to decorate Doris was struck with a moment of genius.

'What about a log burner?' she said.

'But we're putting central heating in,' I said.

'Yes, but it would add character to the room, and it would be insurance against power cuts. We could light it when it's not cold enough for central heating.'

'Just brilliant,' I said.

Photo 12 Doris decorates the living room

Wood burners are hugely popular in rural France, not least because mains gas does not reach the countryside. As electricity is possibly the cheapest in Europe, visitors are often surprised to learn that most French homes have a back up (usually bottled) gas supply. Additionally there will often be a second (gas) hob fitted in the kitchen near to the electric one because electricity supplies are so regularly interrupted. We were not so concerned about the cooking – we had an 'emergency' kitchen in the caravan. Indeed, the caravan was still our only kitchen. All the same, we just had to have a reliable method of keeping some heat in the property before winter flexed its icy claws.

We had considered bottled gas which is racked up in cages at most garages and supermarkets, but this was not the best solution for us. Doris was absolutely right; in Entrechoux many of the houses had their winter woodpiles stacked up alongside, and the surrounding area was heavily wooded. Surely this was the way to go.

We soon learnt that the burners themselves come in all shapes and sizes, but are measured in output. The supplier does a standard calculation based on your general requirements and the size of the room where it is to be installed. It was determined that we needed an 11 kilowatt heater.

Logs generally come pre-cut to size, our load aperture was 54 cm which meant logs were to be cut to 50 cm. I rang around for quotes from wood suppliers. Larger loads are cheaper *pro rata*: so the equation was all to do with storage and seasoning. We bought two lots; one seasoned and ready to burn (relatively pricey), and another which would be ready in 12 to 18 months. Time will tell if we got the quantities right. I also feel that we will find cheaper suppliers – probably a couple of likely lads with chain saws and a white van – in the course of time.

We had been told that the Charente evenings become chill enough for background heating from mid October. We also knew that serious chill would arrive hard on the heels of Santa Claus. We arranged to have the burner delivered in early October and the central heating installed the following month. The cast iron burner came with the ten metres of flexible chimney lining we had ordered. Kevin climbed onto the roof and dropped a length of rope down the chimney. We tied the piping to the rope and up it went. Apart from putting in some packing around the top of the chimney, that was it. Installation complete.

Photo 13 A delivery of logs

Since our arrival in August we had slept in the caravan, but by the beginning of November it was time to move out. We moved into the sitting room to sleep. Electric cables still dangled like black spaghetti from the ceiling and the holes remained in the walls where we had ripped out cupboards.

But it was the floor that took first prize for vile. The timbers had accumulated years of filth and the perfume of dog was ingrained. We knew that the Colditz fence around the back of the property had been erected by the previous owners who bred huskies; we had presumed that Arctic sled dogs would have been happy enough outside. But obviously not. Indeed our neighbour, Bernard, had confirmed that the pack – which was estimated at 21 – spent their evenings indoors.

'The problem, you see *Monsieur*,' he explained, 'is that the husky is an animal more like the horse than the dog. They are good for pulling the sled. They are good for fighting the wolves. But they fill the house with shit.'

Doris has always had the ability to make us comfortable and her sleeping arrangements were immensely practical. Each night we put down a large plastic sheet, on top of this went blankets, camping mattresses and sleeping bags. We were nice and warm because the wood burning stove was now fully operational.

One of our nearest neighbours is a widow called Marie. In the French way of things there is a constant stream of family to see her; as one car leaves another arrives. In the school holidays, there is always a small posse of grandchildren around.

Her house is also warmed by a big log burner. The logs, which are kept in the cellar of a property across the road, invariably arrive on an open wagon driven by her son. The street is so narrow at this point he is unable to turn and back the wagon, so he dumps the lot, as quickly as possible, at the roadside.

The drill then is that the family shift the wood by the barrow load to the storage yard. This year the only hands on deck were the son, his wife, and two teenage boys. I was therefore pressed into service.

It had been a suspension-sagging delivery – a year's supply all at once, so there were half a dozen of us, sleeves rolled up, loading logs into barrows, trundling the barrows to the cellar and tipping, or throwing the logs into the store. As it was more than an hour before the last log was dropped down the hatchway I was absolutely done in.

At some point, during the log shift, Marie spoke to me.

I thought that she said, '*Vous aimez du pain?*'

To which to I replied '*Mais oui, Madame*'.

She promised to bring some the next day and I looked forward to a home-baked delivery.

Sure enough, the next day, there was a knock at the door. Marie and one of her grandchildren were standing there smiling. Marie thanked me again for the help with the logs and the small boy handed me a plastic bag. I took the bag, which was pleasantly warm to the touch, to the void that was the kitchen area, where I opened it. It was a very freshly skinned rabbit.

'You deaf old fart,' said Doris gently. It was never '*du pain*', but '*lapin*'. We should have guessed when we saw her walking down the street this morning. It was half an hour earlier than the normal time she goes to feed the rabbits. That was because it was the rabbit's turn to feed us.'

Doris held the rabbit up to the light.

'And this one's so fresh that if you gave it the kiss of life it could be back on its feet in no time.'

13
Pumpkins and Prices

In the run up to Halloween a friend gave us four pumpkins. As I could only just lift the largest of them, I assumed it was a monster, but not so, the pumpkin aficionados of France are a bit like the show onion-growers in the UK. I read somewhere that the record for a pumpkin in France was 354 kg.

Now it was time for advice. Pumpkin soup came to mind, but we didn't know where to begin, so I hoisted the largest specimen into my arms and took it round to Marie's house. The idea was that this trophy-sized gourd would be a *quid pro quo* for the rabbit and perhaps a little advice on making soup.

I had expected her to invite me in, take the pumpkin with appropriate thanks and share some advice on recipes.

I was already staggering with the strain when she opened the door. She looked at me with mild curiosity, stepped outside, and closed the door. Neither the pumpkin or myself were about to enter the house.

'What do I do with this?' I asked.

She smiled.

'David,' she said, 'why don't you make pumpkin soup?'

And that was it. I had to beat a retreat. Doris had seen me coming and as I reached La Maison D'Etre she opened the door.

'You look just about the same colour as the pumpkin,' she said.

Marie had not been intentionally rude. During late October in France pumpkins are no rarer than falling leaves; market stalls collapse under the weight; supermarket car parks are cluttered with trailer loads of them, and in villages throughout the pumpkin belt children are taught the etiquette of polite refusal.

'Would like some nice big pumpkins?'

'No thank you, *Monsieur*. Our cellar is already bursting and my father will sell me for medical experiments if he can't get his car into the garage.'

Fortunately they take Halloween seriously in the Charente. Almost as soon as it is dark the village children, with their witches' hats and broomsticks, will knock on the door. One of the nice things about living in rural France is that you can still invite the children into your home, say admiring things about their costumes, and give them some sweets.

And there are pumpkin lanterns everywhere.

The two smaller pumpkins became festive illumination and the third we gave to my son, Simon, who had a large car boot and, as a recent immigrant, had not yet learnt pumpkin refusal etiquette.

Which left us only with the problem of the fourth – the monster.

We had some English friends nearby who had given us some pumpkin jam in exchange for feeding their ducks when they were away on holiday.

'I'll get the recipe from them,' said Doris.

'And I'll type 'pumpkin' into Google and see what turns up,' I said. And that was it. By the end of the week Doris had prepared pumpkin jam, pumpkin pie, pumpkin stew, pumpkin rissoles, pumpkin relish and pumpkin soup. We ate the soup, packed the jam and relish on shelves and shoe-horned the rest into the freezer.

'And if you are offered pumpkins next year, what do you say?' asked Doris.

'I say that our cellar is full and that if you can't get the car into the garage you'll sell me for medical experiments.'

'Nasty ones,' she said.

By now we were convinced that day-to-day living in France is much cheaper than the UK.

We have no mortgage, which when compared to the loan we paid off before we moved here, makes a huge difference, and not only are local taxes lower, I also get an age reduction of 20%. Furthermore because of age and income we do not have to have a TV licence (which is incorporated into *taxe d'habitation* and then discounted).

Everything you earn in France is taxed in France which, happily, was not a consideration for us, but for some people it can be a problem. Our occupational pensions as teachers are taxed in the UK. Indeed this rule applies to any pension earned as a former Government employee. Our state pensions however are taxed in France. If we had private pension annuities or income from a share portfolio, this would also fall into the net of French income tax. The French tax system is geared in favour of large families with children under the age of 18. If we had to pay most of our income tax in France we would perhaps pay more than in the UK. Set against this is the fact that allowances can be claimed in both countries. We are certain we are better off as a result.

It is difficult to compare electricity costs for a three bedroom UK semi and a much larger property in France. Considering we have twice as many radiators and have been running power tools, including cement mixers and auxiliary lighting, I do not think the bills have been outrageous. Certainly the price per unit in France for electricity remains lower than in the UK.

We had found a superb local restaurant. Everything about the establishment – the décor, service, and presentation are top class. Best of all a five course lunch with as much wine as you want comes out at €13 per head.

Shop prices for food are very similar to the UK but, of course, a great deal of what is destined for the table is bought at local markets. This is not always particularly cheap, but the quality is invariably good and, of course, there are seasonal bargains. Meat is quite pricey but again the quality is good. Even the humble beef burger can be 100% beef.

Whereas retail price maintenance has long gone in the UK – other than the way it is allegedly operated by cartels – it is still alive and well in France. Prices are fixed – and published – by manufacturers and producers which means, in theory, you will pay the same price for the same item wherever it is sold. But, of course, that does not quite happen. What does happen is that, according to certain rules, discounts can be applied. These discounts, however, are invariably smaller when applied to branded goods.

I have never particularly liked the idea of branded goods. There is something very cow's backside and red hot iron about it. Anyway, you may think you are buying the brand but the brand is branding you. So you have that nice swish on your sweat shirt? Yes, you are now part of the herd.

Unbranded or own branded goods in France find their own market level. They compete essentially on price and quality and in this case it is the customer's reliance on the retailer that is most important. For most of our regular shopping we go to Leader Price who sell mainly their own range of goods. We have done our comparisons carefully: a full shopping trolley is almost exactly 20% cheaper than at our local supermarket.

Store sales (*soldes*) in France are also different. For a start they have to be 'real' sales which means that the goods, by law, are discounted at various rates up to 40% of normal retail prices. That price must be the real up-to-date retail price in the store – not some higher retail price that has notionally been charged in a sister store up to 28 days earlier.

It works like this: we bought carpets from a reputable retailer. As we chose to buy two identical patterned carpets of different sizes they were both discounted by 40%. The reason for the discount? Well, both had been on display for more than six months and French law says that when a 'sale' is declared the discount, in those circumstances, will be 40%. This may sound prescriptive and it is. It also means that French people trust sale notices: a sale is genuinely a sale and the queues at the shop doors prove it.

Many second homes in France – used essentially during the warmer months – do not have central heating. Where this occurs the most popular option for water heating is the electric immersion heater because there is no need to remove fumes through a flue or duct. As we had gone for the wood burning stove to create background heat we gave this brief consideration, but winter temperatures in the Charente made it a non starter.

As we always like to explore the 'green' option we considered heat pump technology. This will ultimately be the way to go. It is said that a heat pump can take four times as much energy from the air as it uses in electricity – four kilowatts to one is quite an equation. The trouble is that installation costs are still high and there are problems associated with servicing, especially in a rural area.

The French often claim that the best and cheapest heating system is wall-mounted convectors. To be efficient, very high levels of insulation are required – such as that which can be found in new apartment blocks. This system was certainly was not right for La Maison d'Etre.

Gas-fired heating is another popular option, particularly in urban areas where town gas is available, but for most people gas means installing a propane tank, and propane is both more volatile and expensive than oil. We considered gas because it allows the installation of a white boiler with a balanced flue in the kitchen without the cooking smells from the oven mixing with the background aroma of a garage forecourt. But we went for oil, or more literally industrial diesel. Oil boilers in France are very expensive, but again it's more like driving a Jaguar than a Suzuki. The power output is everything you need, in all conditions, and with more than a little to spare. In truth we never had much say in this, but have not regretted the choice. Kevin had firm ideas about what was best. He also had 14 years' experience as a builder out here, and on this he has been proved absolutely right.

Oil fired heating is the market leader in France. The heating unit can be either floor or wall mounted and it is claimed that the latest condensing technology can save up to 20% in energy costs. Boilers require plenty of space for ventilation and larger boilers are considered best for stone built houses as the larger boiler heats and cools less rapidly – a more suitable option when used with cast iron radiators.

In a large house like La Maison D'Etre, the hard work comes from fitting the piping. We got a good deal on a boiler from the *Brico Dépôt* in Poitiers: 20 radiators, and more than 75 metres of copper piping. Kevin and I worked together on the fitting and then I insulated the lot. As it was a diesel system, we also had to buy a tank which holds 1,200 litres, which seems to last us around nine months. We set the tank into a bed of well mixed sand and cement but no water (Kevin's idea again). If there is no water, the tank moulds itself into the bed and hardens slowly as it soaks up moisture from the air.

It was now well into November and the nights were decidedly cold. We were making progress, but slowly – this was at least partly because Kevin had family problems.

When all the radiators and pipes were fitted and lagged there was a final snag: Kevin was not qualified to commission the boiler. But, of course, he knew a man who was. Unhappily, *Monsieur* Fouquet had a full time job, so it was arranged that he would do ours one weekend. It turned out it was to be two weeks before he arrived and it was a week after that before the work was complete.

It was a moment of high anxiety. Imagine, if you like, taking a brand new war ship out of harbour for her sea trials. Millions has been spent on building all the systems, but you do not know if they are going to work until you throw the switches.

It was Saturday night on the 4th of December at 21.00 hours. I was stressed, Doris was stressed, Kevin was super-stressed because he had promised to take his wife out to dinner that night. But *Monsieur* Fouquet was super-mega-stressed. He had not expected to work so late and had nervously been firing off texts to both his wife and girlfriend. He was also fairly drunk because we had made the mistake of making our beer supplies rather too accessible.

The system was fired up and we waited. There was the odd rumbling and then it went quiet: could it really be as simple as that? We divided the house into zones and each went off looking for leaks. Nothing. We came together in the living room and cracked open the last of the beer in celebration.

We spent Christmas 2003 in England. The plan was to see as many of our grandchildren as possible.

In spite of having had my 'flu jab in France I picked up a cold. This surprised me as I have had a winter 'flu jab for years now and it has always done the trick. This time I was unlucky, and even though they say that all life's greatest pleasures begin with 's' – like sugar and sleep – I am not sure that sneezing and snot should be added to the list.

In England you turn up at the surgery, they give you a little prick and off you go.

Not in France. This would be far too straightforward. As a male over 65 I automatically received through the mail one letter and two prescriptions. The letter explained my entitlement in just 20 paragraphs. In essence, prescription one allowed me to see a doctor free of charge. Prescription two was for the vaccine.

I went to the doctor who took the first prescription from me and signed the second, which I took to the pharmacy to collect the vaccine. I was instructed to put it in a fridge, which presumably proves conclusively that people who do not own fridges are more likely to catch 'flu. Then I made another doctor's appointment. After perusing the paperwork the doctor gave me the jab. Now, although this was technically 'free', it actually cost €20 which I had to pay before leaving the surgery. At the same time I collected another form from the receptionist. It took me no more than a couple of hours to understand this, fill it in, and return to the surgery with it. There it was countersigned and dispatched to the appropriate state ministry with prescription one attached to it. And finally, several weeks later the ministry reimbursed the €20 to my bank account. Simple isn't it?

For me the jury is still out on whether the French really are the best when it comes to *la vie sexuelle*. There is no doubt however that when it comes to a lust for pieces of paper they are insatiable.

Just as you think you have a system sorted, the bureaucrats spring a fresh surprise. One of these is that you now have to be registered with a doctor if you want to be reimbursed the full cost of house calls. First you fill in a form saying which doctor you fancy. Or, if you prefer, you can select a doctor on the basis of their competence. In practice, of course, it usually comes down to choosing someone local.

The idea, of course, is to save money. The snag is, it goes against the grain with the French. If they are told they eat or drink too much they want a second opinion and, if the second opinion is the same as the first, they want a third. Consequently, although a nice new bureaucracy has been set up to manage the claims and payments for the new system, many people have refused to sign up to it. It is therefore not cost effective.

I think this begins to explain why the French Health Service is deeper in the doody than my *fosse septique*. But there is definitely an upside: in French hospitals you get a glass of wine with your dinner!

14

Hardcore and the Five Feeds

The first job of 2004 was fitting out the bedroom where Doris and I were to sleep; it had an *en suite* bathroom and would be very nice when finished. We had always liked the look of authentic French style furniture and a local store had a sale, so off we went.

They had two wardrobes in the style that we wanted and they were massive. We had not realised that they came as flat packs – they looked so solid. They fortunately arrived with a couple of big lads. Between us we struggled upstairs with them. All we had to do now was put them up.

Flat packs in France are no better and no worse than in England. We finally got them finished and into position – one at each end of our bedroom which measures nine metres by four without the *en suite*. We could never have afforded a house with rooms this size in the UK. Anything less than king-sized wardrobes would have been lost in there. It was quite wonderful.

The whites and yellow blooms of the early Spring were already giving way to a tapestry of colour. *Monsieur* Crochet had returned to his seat on the village green and we still did not have a kitchen.

Doris had been cooking in the caravan for eight months now – even managing to prepare meals for friends, but enough was enough. We had to begin the process by filling in the cellar. For some reason Kevin seemed reluctant to get the 30 tons of hardcore from the farm where it had long been stored.

We resorted first to threats and then blackmail. When he saw that the task was inevitable he arranged for the farmer to load his truck. The idea was that we'd shovel it in together.

He had a battered blue truck and on the appointed day he arrived and parked it alongside the kitchen window. I'd already taken the glass frames out as a precaution.

With the side of the truck down we stood side by side – one each side of the window. It took about half an hour to empty the load, and, because we were swinging alternatively, I had to keep pace with Kevin. He was exhausted and I was twice his age. I now knew why he had been reluctant to move the hardcore.

It took three days to get all 30 tons into the cellar. I then had to try and spread it out evenly. This is not like putting jam on bread. It's more like trying to flatten off the top of a mountain. Kevin left me to it as he claimed there were greater demands on his expertise. He was putting the finishing touches to the kitchen electrics which basically amounted to putting in the electric feeds, which in turn would be buried under four inches of concrete.

The greatest pain of all this was not in my back but my wallet. The final cost of the work was closer to £2,000 than the 'ballpark' £500 he had estimated.

Kevin and I were now both working on the kitchen electrics. New arrivals in France often complain about the system being different but, on reflection, it's the UK who are out of step as the rest of Europe do their wiring like the French. You could, of course, wire your house 'English Style', but you might have problems with an insurance claim in the event of a fire because the ring main system used in the UK is illegal in France. The French method is to have separate circuits running from the main electrical source to each socket group and back again. The standard (or norm) is defined by NFC 15 100 which is a precise specification for trip switch (ratings), cable sizes and power outlets (per circuit) for various kinds of appliances.

We also found out why installing a new supply is expensive. La Maison D'Etre had the kind of cotton-wrapped cable I'd not seen in England since the 1950s, and the lighting in our old shower room used 'speaker' wire.

If the French sometimes seem rather cavalier in this respect I think it is because they were brought up on the old 120 volt system which meant you could take more liberties with it. Indeed the rule remains that you can patch up an old system *ad infinitum* without permission but if you put in a new system you have to go through planning.

We have friends who bought three old houses for renovation, all without electricity. A little more surprising, perhaps, was that quite a few of the inhabited houses in the same village did not have a supply either. We were told that, in one house, an old lady, goes up to bed via outside steps. In winter she carries a candle lamp.

This is by no means unusual. There are still many people in France who manage, apparently quite happily, without electricity. Perhaps there is another reason for this; we know of a family who were recently quoted €3,000 just to be connected and this was in a hamlet where there was already a mains supply. The second problem they faced was that all the wiring in the house had to be completed and inspected before they were connected.

Finally the cellar was filled in. The pipes for water and electricity were installed. The next stage was cementing, but we had no cement.

'It's our top priority now,' I told Kevin, 'so please order the cement.'

'I will,' he said, but he did nothing.

A few days later I decided to phrase it more firmly.

'If you don't order the cement I cannot be responsible for what Doris might do to you.'

That did the trick.

'OK, it will be here on Thursday,' he said.

There was quite a lot of preparation to do before Thursday. The area of the cellar was 23 square yards which was to be filled to around four inches with cement. That was a lot of cement to put down quickly so we needed to mark the fill lines carefully.

Fortunately Kevin had a new toy – a laser-levelling device which gave us a blue line right around the cellar. The next thing was to put down a plastic membrane and top this off with wire meshing for reinforcement. All that remained now was to work out how to get the cement into the cellar. The plan was to point the driver down the side of the house to the kitchen window which would have to be removed again, but putting the cement in there would mean we could work nicely from the middle of the floor outwards.

Thursday arrived. The cement was promised for 9.30am but at 10 there was still no cement. Kevin made a phone call.

'Good news,' he said, 'the load would be here by 11. Don't look so disbelieving. Look, I'm saying 'Ready mix' without my fingers crossed behind my back.'

The driver arrived at 11.15 and managed to manoeuvre the cement mixer to the kitchen window. But that was no good, the window was slightly up and the delivery chute had to go down. The only option now was to shove the cement straight in through the door – which meant starting at the corner of the room. This would make spreading it around with rakes more difficult.

Kevin explained our problem and asked for a nice smooth slow delivery. The driver responded with an insouciant smile and proceeded to dump the whole lot down the chute at once.

We fell all over the place as we raked. The wire mesh under the wellies did not help as they made each fall a lottery; you never knew quite how much damage to yourself you were doing. The longer we worked the heavier the cement became to work and the more it clung to every inch of our overalls and skin. In the end we must have looked like slow motion aliens working in a sea of grey sludge.

Towards the end of this I looked up and wiped my eyes. I had expected the driver to be long gone but he was looking down at us with barely concealed mirth. Kevin had seen him too. Later I imagined his conversation when he returned to the depot.

'You know, Pierre, I delivered to the English this morning. A full mixer. The big mixer.'

'And did you dump it all at once, François?'

'Naturally, it was very funny. Better than the circus I think.'

Kevin wanted to be away. It seemed to me that the cement was not level but he said it would settle OK and off he went. By now I was exhausted and there were still tools to clean up. I consoled myself with the fact that we now had a kitchen floor, waste water disposal pipes and electrics.

The next day Kevin and I inspected the floor.

'You know I'm sure I put five electric feeds down but I can only find four,' he said.

So we inspected the floor again. One, two three, four. Not five. Positively not five.

'I don't make mistakes,' he said, 'there were definitely five. It must be down there somewhere,' he said.

'Yes,' I said, 'but so is 30 tons of rubble, metal reinforcement and four inches of concrete.'

The regulations on the number of sockets per feed are very specific. Worse still, if you overload a feed and later try to claim on insurance, you could find the policy is invalid. We needed all five feeds for the kitchen to function as planned.

'Well, I suppose the floor will have to come up,' he said, 'pity really, we'd made rather a good job of it.'

Doris had joined us by now and had quickly read the situation. She had gone ashen white and for a moment I thought she was going to pass out.

'It's not going to happen,' I said, 'we'll just have to manage somehow.'

We made ourselves a coffee and began to work out a compromise that could still, legally, give us the minimum number of sockets we needed. It was less than ideal and it was also bitterly disappointing. In fact it was a total cock up.

'Well,' said Kevin, 'maybe if you water the floor a few times the missing feed will come up.'

I believe that Doris and I are reasonable, even generous people. Certainly, with the possible exception of Adolf Hitler, we have never felt that murder is justified, but the pick axe was leaning against the wall and Doris was leaning on a shovel. Kevin will never know how close he came to being featured under the tabloid headline 'Builder Brutally Slain by Pensioners'.

15
The Case of
the Missing Tiles

We had now made up our minds that Kevin had to go. He had become increasingly unreliable and had already taken a big chunk of our contingency cash.

It had been partly our own fault. We had deviated from the *devis* and had paid him up front on the hourly rate. The result was a £4,000 black hole – largely for work that we could have done ourselves or could have left until later. The last straw had been the concreting of the kitchen floor: it had taken for ever to get him to do it and then he'd clearly forgotten to imbed some leads and connections. He had made similar mistakes in wiring lights in the main downstairs room. Anything that has to be done twice is twice as expensive and we just couldn't take it any more.

He wasn't at all surprised to be given the sack. There was a kind of natural rationale to it. Kevin simply took on more and more work until each of his employers, in turn, got rid of him. Meanwhile, of course, he found new people to work for – invariably British. More people to make a mug of. More pockets to pick.

Kevin did not contest our decision. He smiled, finished his sandwich, packed up his gear and went.

Looking back we have mixed feelings about him. He was

unreliable, untruthful, and he overcharged, but he could also be immensely practical, even inspiring. He also, partly by default, gave us the confidence to tackle jobs that seemed beyond us. Although we were not sorry to see him go I am not sure we would have made so much progress without him, nor would we have learned half as much.

We decided on large tiles for the kitchen floor. As they had a sale on at our local *bricolage*, we went to try our luck. We chose a pattern we liked with some matching edgings and went to place our order. We needed ten packs, the computer stock list said they only had seven. It would take two weeks to order the extra packs. We paid a deposit and left.

We called after the fortnight: no tiles, in fact no record of the order. Same arrangement: telephone in a fortnight. Two weeks later, still no tiles, but two weeks after that – a minor miracle – our tiles had arrived.

We arrived in a downpour, ran into the building and were asked to wait. We waited 20 minutes and at the end of that time we had pretty much stopped dripping on the floor, but there were still no tiles. The cashier offered us *bricolage* brochures to read.

Doris suggested that with their level of efficiency they might consider keeping a few novels.

We could hear the buzz of argument in the background. The manager was saying that they were on the computer stock list and therefore they had them, while the lad in the yard was suggesting that the computer might like to come outside into the rain to try to find them.

The manager went into the yard and returned five minutes later looking determined but moist. He checked his stock list again and barked further instructions into the yard. Less than a minute later we heard a triumphal cheer.

Our tiles, although incorrectly labelled, had been found.

The soaking wet boxes disintegrated as we loaded the tiles into our trailer and as we drove home we could hear the load moving. I pulled over immediately but some tiles were already broken.

We considered our options and decided to leave Doris with the trailer whilst I loaded as many as possible into the car. We would have to transport them in shifts. But then, a stroke of luck. One of neighbours came past with an empty jeep and we loaded the remaining tiles into the back.

Despite the fact it had failed us this time I would recommend buying a trailer to anyone buying a country property in France. Even a medium-sized French garden produces a lot of weeds and grass cuttings, and when it comes to renovation there is bound to be a lot of stripped out material and rubble. Then there are the trips to the *bricolage* and builders' merchants.

Our trailer is plated for a maximum payload of 500 kilos and reputable builders' merchants will not fill it beyond that limit. Even the sand hopper has a metre which indicates the weight of each load. 500 kilos may seem a fair whack, but its not very much in sand and cement.

Older village properties in the Charente are invariably stone built and, as renovation projects progress, people either have a deficit or surplus of stone. We wanted to build some low level garden walls so, whenever we were driving around, we played 'spot the surplus', then it was hitch up the trailer and go and collect it.

One problem is that stone, despite being heavy, throws itself around the trailer and this constant change of balance is very scary when you are driving. I overcame this with what I hope to patent as 'the device which means you don't have to wear brown trousers when you're pulling a trailer full of stone'. It works like this: using suitable planks I made a removable cross-shape division in the trailer – creating four compartments. Loading a similar amount of stone into each compartment massively reduces stone movement and keeps the trailer nicely balanced. Wonderful. Like all great inventions it is both brilliant and simple.

16 – The Mouse Trap

Having survived a short, sharp winter we were surprised to find just how quickly the spring weather changed the landscape. In some ways it was not so very different from the UK, but in the Charente we felt the rule of Texas applies: everything is bigger, brighter, and better. If you own a vernacular building there is also the heightened sense of communion.

We have friends who have converted an old mill nearby with some of the old mechanisms still functioning; they were surrounded by the rhythm of water and the movement and music of wildlife, but they also have snakes. One Christmas morning they woke to find six in the kitchen. The fact that nature moves indoors in the cool season is also unheralded by estate agents.

There had been a mouse or two in the caravan during the winter. We had no idea how they were getting in until we spotted one climbing the piece of wood we had kept wedged in the door to allow air to circulate. Clearly this was their access ramp.

Bats were welcome, but mice were a different matter. They are not cuddly little British field mice, these are the Arnold Schwarzeneggers of the rodent world. They don't just nibble through paper, they go through heavy, waxed card cartons lined with metal foil. At one point we were losing several UHT milk litre packs a week. We put down poison but it just seemed to bolster their biceps.

So we went to *Monsieur Bricolage* – the French equivalent of
B & Q – and looked at traps. As we preferred rodent removal to
murder we bought one with an elaborate patchwork of entrances
and trapdoors which cost £15. We packed it with ripe cheeses,
chocolate and honey. The bait disappeared but so did the mice.

'Our only hope,' I said, 'is that they will grow so fat that they can't
get out.'

Back to *Monsieur Bricolage* and a similar but smaller trap; a snip at
just £8.

Kevin had used an interesting technique for mitreing corners. The
problem is – say you're doing a picture frame – that when you
hammer in the nails, the edges move out of line. The answer is to
use a fine nail that fits into the chuck of a cordless drill. You drill
through the mitred corners just far enough into the wood, hammer
in the nails and the joints stay where they should. I used this
technique when setting the mouse trap. The cheese and chocolate
were threaded with cotton and the cotton was tied to the spring
mechanism. It worked; the first morning we found five contented
but incarcerated mice. We collected a couple of dozen during the
first week and after a fortnight there were no more.

But a few days later another carton of UHT milk was raided. It
occurred to me that the mice that I had released on the other side
of the Odorat were returning. Bernard, our neighbour, suggested
branding them. I didn't like the idea much until he pointed out
that this could be accomplished with lipstick. I gave it some
thought but decided this was impractical. In the first place how
would you get them to purse their lips?

The next bunch of captives went straight into the Odorat.

'Don't worry,' said Doris, 'they can swim.'

I decided not to mention Bernard's cat which had been prowling
on the opposite bank downstream.

17
A Harley at the Party

Our new builder was Ricky – a swarthy, moustachioed Scouser whose torso was a pattern book for tattoo art. We promised him two days' work a week, agreed an hourly rate and confirmed that we would provide the materials.

We had already become close friends with his parents – Margaret and Ted – who admitted that just about their only preparation for coming to France was to watch a few episodes of 'A *Place in the Sun*' on television. They did, however, have the advantage of having an immensely resourceful son.

It may be they could have succeeded anyway as their attitude is entirely positive. But we have also witnessed disasters, which invariably begin with a rose tinted view of life in France.

I think there is a connection to the phenomenon that UK marketing men call '*nouveau rustique*'. I understand that this refers to the kind of British family who quit the city in search of a chocolate box, sweet-smelling, machinery-free countryside. The move is often born from a messianic commitment to a safer environment (and better schools for their children), clean country air and communion with nature. In order to achieve this dream, they immediately push into spheres of influence such as the parish council, the WI, and the steering committee for the Village Green Preservation Society.

This dream may have some credence in the Cotswolds but rural France is different. French villages with tea rooms, scented candle gifts shops, and post offices selling booklets of local farm walks do not exist and the French are less than delighted when outsiders move in and try to take over local institutions. Indeed the British start with a disadvantage – they are foreigners, they do not understand the French way of life, and by creating enclaves they may be pushing up local property values beyond the means of the French locals. At least that is the perception.

To make things worse we have also seen British insensitivity at its worst. It may be based on ignorance or a lack of respect, or it may imply a lack of preparation and an unwillingness, or even an inability, to integrate. In the end it is usually something apparently trivial which sparks the Briton into putting up the 'for sale' sign. We know of one classic case where a tap started leaking and the property owner had neither the ability to either deal with it personally or to communicate the problem to a French plumber. If you feel like a stranger in a foreign land you will always be so; it is both an attitude and a state of mind.

As we had found out, there is also the steep learning curve of unscrupulous estate agents, dodgy builders and so on. And, looking back, we had probably made another potentially fatal mistake. Viewing property in the spring is much less sensible than looking at the middle of winter. Oddly enough French estate agencies don't tell you that anywhere within the pull of the Massif Centrale – and all our target area qualified – can be bitterly cold for a few weeks each winter. Temperatures can easily fall to minus 16 degrees at night, but that is not the full story. Your insurance does not cover an unoccupied property where the pipes freeze, and there can even be a clause which insists, that in certain conditions, you should drain all water flow systems – including the toilet.

Meeting Ricky for the first time was a touch disconcerting. His sunny smile is the perfect adjunct to his tightly cropped hair, tattoos and pierced ears. At first the signals were mixed – I suppose we did not know what to expect. As it turned out Ricky is one of the nicest people you could meet and, better still, he proved to be an honest, reliable and intelligent builder. The slightly surprising thing was he had not come to France to follow this vocation, his ambition was to start a specialist art business.

On his 40th birthday Ricky bought himself a Harley Davison and hired the local *salle de fête* for the evening. There was music, dancing, lots to eat, and rather too much to drink. The highlight of the evening was hearing the roar of the Harley as he rode it, out of the October darkness, right into the *salle de fête*.

At first people did not know how to react. Then it was the Mayor, *Monsieur* Cabacou, who led the applause.

Early in the New Year my son, Simon, had sent out a digibox, LNB and satellite dish. The system had waited patiently in boxes for a little TV electrical know-how. It took Ricky just a couple of hours to install it.

The Free Sat package included all the UK mainstream terrestrials. Basically we got the BBC and ITV output plus Sky News and a dozen or so channels of dross which compete for unwatchability. If pushed, my vote for the very worst would go to the Lunn Poly channel. Beyond this you need a UK address for subscription services. Once we began to get notices that ITV transmissions would end I contacted Simon again. He sent out a new Free Sat card which cost a one-off £27 and it seems to have done the trick. The bonus is access to UK radio stations. There is something quite blissful about putting your feet up in the French winter sunshine and listening to road reports – particularly when the M25 is hit by the first flurries of snow. One trick is to output the satellite signal through a hi-fi system so you don't have to turn your TV monitor on. Better still, if you have a home cinema system with wireless speakers, you can carry Terry Wogan and Alan Green out into the garden with you.

Ricky's next job was to help me finish the kitchen, which meant levelling off the floor, plastering the walls, panelling the back wall, putting in a cupboard for electrics and then assembling the flat pack units.

It was surprising how quickly all this was achieved. Working alongside someone who turns up on time and gets on with the job, was strangely energising.

Photo 14 The kitchen: a work in progress

The floor was up to four centimetres out in the worst places, so we put down self levelling compound. It was easy to use, we just poured it out and went away to let it settle. Job done.

Ricky and I plastered the kitchen using a method different from the one I had learnt from Kevin. Standard French *plâtre* (plaster) comes in two grades – 3,000 and 2,000 and he used the latter on our walls.

Like mixing most plasters, the water goes in first, then you need an electric drill with a twirler on the end – like a food mixer. You mix to a consistency where you can hold the bucket upside down and the plaster does not fall out. Then you simply float it onto the wall like porridge. Better still, you can even come back next day to get rid of marks and runs. You just damp the surface down with a spray and rework. The same method is also good for filling.

We also worked on the other jobs together, but I left Ricky to build the kitchen units. In his previous UK incarnation he had worked as manager for a company making doors and windows. This was his *métier*.

The fashion in French kitchens has moved from completely fitted to a more free-standing look which is, at least partly, because of the possible build up of damp at the back of fitted units.

Photo 15 The completed kitchen

It is often claimed that local joiners can do a better and cheaper job than building a flat pack. That may well be true, but the problem is finding the joiner who is better and cheaper. Getting the attention of a real craftsman, who comes personally recommended is not easy. We had tried a couple; they came, saw, promised to give a detailed quote, and then disappeared from public view as completely as Lord Lucan. This had persuaded us to take the flat pack route. We had bought ours in England because we had heard that French units, and therefore worktops, were lower than English ones. Our one worry was that there would be something missing

105

and our units were probably deleted stock by now and, even if it was possible, the thought of getting something sent out by an English supplier was pretty daunting.

That aside, fitting a kitchen is, relatively, one of the easier DIY jobs. One of the important things is not to make the units too airtight. If the walls on which they are mounted cannot breathe, the damp can set in very quickly. And when chipboard starts to swell and sag the only remedy is a bonfire. It is also worth remembering that French water systems are under constant mains pressure, although a pressure reduction valve is sometimes fitted near the water meter. The point is that one careless hammer blow can turn the kitchen floor into a lagoon and when it is a nice new kitchen floor, this is best avoided.

As Ricky built the units, I took out the fireplace which had been the seat of the celebrated fire which occurred when the Germans left. This left a gaping hole approximately two metres by three which I filled with concrete blocks. In the UK these appear to be used mainly as internal wall materials, while in France they normally use traditional bricks in the north and concrete blocks in the south. As we lived pretty much in the centre I felt I could make an executive decision.

The blocks usually come in three sizes; all are 50 centimetres long and 20 centimetres wide with depths of 10, 15, or 20 centimetres. The rough rule of thumb is the higher the wall the thicker the block. For the fireplace I decided the 10 centimetre size would do.

I used two spirit levels, one 60 cm long and one a metre and a half. The short one I used to keep the present block level and the longer one to make sure the rows were level vertically and horizontally. I checked diagonally across the rows as well. I know from bitter experience that, once out of true, it is difficult to put things right again. To make sure, I only did two rows at a time.

Working on the fireplace I used a mortar mix of four sand to one of cement which I mixed initially on a large piece of wood, then added the water a little at a time. After a couple of mixes I knew how much water to put in the bucket and then, following the dry mix, I sloshed in most of the water immediately. This is hard work. When I need a larger quantity of mortar I mix in the wheelbarrow. For really big jobs, a concrete mixer is the best preventative of backache.

The gap that had once been the fireplace was something of a pyramid shape. After the first two rows, I had to cut the blocks at either end with a diamond disc angle grinder to make them fit.

There are some great deals on tools in France. In Entrechoux an *Outiror* van comes round once a month or so. We get a flyer through the letter box telling us where and when, and it pays to get there early. The *Outiror* – which is about the size of a mobile library – is a magnet to DIY aficionados. I have seen them huddling in groups in a winter storm waiting for the van to arrive.

Outiror sell an amazing range of DIY goods, gardening, and household items. All the items are reasonably priced, while some are unbelievably cheap. I bought a holdall containing three different sized angle grinders plus 10 different discs for less than £20. There is a quality issue: what is good enough for an amateur like me would be no good for a professional builder. I'll use an angle grinder once every couple of months, but a builder might use it every day. My bargain is the builder's cash down the drain.

Outiror also give some amazing offers to regular customers. You do not have to buy to claim them and they will post them out to you. Astonishing.

18
The *Auf Wiedersehen* Builders

There is a building attached to the house which we had always called 'the barn'. It was a large, valuable storage area and pretty much all the equipment we needed for building and gardening only filled one small corner. Books and furniture had been gradually relocated and another area was packed with outdoor furniture and barbecue equipment. There were also the tools and furnishings that we had 'inherited' – some of which, given time, may be worthy of cleaning up for use, sale, or as museum pieces. These included some venerable brass instruments which appeared to be of military origin. I had already dusted off the telescope and it appeared to work admirably.

For us 'Let's put it in the barn' had become a way of doing things that was not so much a rationale as a necessity. Only when everything else was finished could we perhaps think of other plans for this area. Our priority in the short term was to do something about the roof, part of which had been blown off in a winter gale a few years earlier.

The problem was that the more we used the barn as a store the more we lost things. This was at least partly because everything had, of necessity, to be covered with tarpaulins. Even the boxes of roofing slates which had been delivered at some point remained anonymous under their waterproof coat. We asked Kevin to get on the job a number of times and certainly he had been paid for his efforts at least twice. The fact remained, though, that the only possible benefit of the roof in its present condition was that if I set up the telescope on its tripod, the barn would make an excellent celestial observatory.

We thought about asking Ricky. He was certainly willing enough, but roofing is a specialist team job and Ricky was primarily a joiner. Besides which we were already throwing more at him than he could keep up with.

Local friends suggested that we used their builders for this project.

'They are both reasonable and hard working,' claimed Angela.

'Then let's have the phone number,' said Doris.

So I called Bob the builder.

'Tuesday,' he said, 'and I'll bring the lads with me.'

The 'lads' were ringers for the *Auf Wiedersehen* mob. Bob was the stocky, balding foreman-type through whom all meaningful conversation was routed, Ossie was a tall and wiry Geordie with a nose that had obviously had several uncomfortable collisions, and Pete – who seemed to be constructed of concentric circles – had an unfathomable Wolverhampton twang. Pete admitted – or at least Bob translated – that after two years in France he had learned almost nothing of the language; worse still, the natives seemed to have problems understanding his dialect which they perhaps assumed to be more Black Sea than Black Country.

'We have to get the work done quickly,' I explained, 'we have children and grandchildren visiting soon.'

'I understand,' said Bob.

'Aye Hinny,' said Ossie.

'Awlright von oirkid,' said Pete.

'And so when can you start?' I asked.

'Right away,' said Bob.

'Noo Hinny,' said Ossie.

'Stray Taway,' said Pete.

And that was it. They stripped off their shirts, ran out their ladders, and by tea time had removed the last vestiges of old tiling.

'Well done lads,' I said, 'tomorrow?'

'Sorry Gaffer,' said Bob, 'it will have to be Saturday.'

'But the forecast is for storms,' I protested.

'Saturday,' said Bob.

'First thing?' I asked hopefully.

'First thing.'

Saturday came, but by ten o'clock there were no builders. I telephoned Bob.

'You promised first thing,' I said.

'Not me,' he said, 'just Ossie and Peter.'

'But they're not here.'

'Are you sure?'

'Unless they're working silently and invisibly.'

'But they should be there. I'll ring you back in 20 minutes.'

Two hours later he telephoned.

They'll be there first thing tomorrow. Five o'clock start.'

'I won't be awake.'

'You will be when they start drilling tiles.'

Next morning by the time I staggered out of the house with a coffee the lads were already at work. In the half light I thought I was seeing double – Ossie and Peter were up on the roof on one side with two near clones working opposite.

First they wanted coffee, then a spirit level, then a pencil.

'A pencil?' I asked.

'Aye, a pencil Hinny,' said Ossie.

Doris had come out to join Ricky and me on the lawn.

'It's almost unbelievable,' she said, 'four builders and not a pencil between them.'

'That's not the half of it,' said Ricky, 'they have already borrowed my scaffolding and drill.'

The job was straightforward, but time consuming. Roofing construction can vary considerably in the Charente and, as the La Maison D'Etre was an older property with a traditional slate roof, the beams had to be carefully embedded first and then covered with layers of wooden 'slates' which were then coated with a waterproof layer – we used a product called Spanflex – before the outer tiling could begin.

We had costed another possible method using 'uppers' and 'overs' – tiles which can be used for both the inner and outer layer. This, however, would have meant the pile of tiles we already had were useless, which seemed to us a terrible waste.

We later learnt of a third method: to lay down corrugated metal strips over the beams and then use a single layer of outer tiles which would have saved us money and had the long term advantage of having the corrugated structure in place for rapid tile replacement if the winter wind caused some mischief. The main disadvantage of this method is a relative lack of insulation, although this would hardly have mattered in the barn. If this had been part of the living accommodation, we could have used an *isolent mince* – a fine gauge insulation. This is around 25 mm in thickness and is most frequently used behind tongue and groove, plasterboard, or the tricky areas you find around dormer windows. Plasterboard backed with insulating material, or polystyrene panels (which can be made to clip into position) are further options. If these materials are used it is important to have roof vents for ventilation. It is also possible to integrate an insulator such as *laine de roche* or *laine de verre* (rockwool or glasswool) into a finished surface. These materials, which come as semi-rigid panels, can also be tacked under the rafters. Whatever approach is taken it is important to treat the timbers in advance.

The job took a week. At the end of it they disassembled Ricky's scaffolding and offered to put it in his van. He was so dumbstruck that he helped them to do it.

After they had left I found a ring in the bathroom. Obviously one of the men had taken it off to scrub his hands so I made enquiries.

It was Ossie who turned up the next day and I handed him the ring as we stood in the street gazing up at the roof. He seemed almost surprised at what he was seeing.

'Well,' he said, 'so it's still there then.'

19
French Kissing

Monsieur Crochet had also enjoyed the tiling.

'I like the sound of the hammer,' he said, 'there is a syncopated rhythm. Like jazz.'

Another sprightly octogenarian (there must be something in the water here) had joined him on the green. This was the former *Madame* Crochet. Appropriately enough she had her knitting on her knees.

'Do you share your husband's enthusiasm for jazz?' I asked.

'I cannot say, *Monsieur*,' she answered, 'I do not talk to him, since the divorce.'

She spoke the word 'divorce' with a hiss, then spat on both her hands and rubbed them together.

I knew something of the history of their troubles. The Crochets had apparently been approaching their golden wedding harmoniously enough when he insisted that he should now be allowed to take a mistress.

'In France,' he said, 'it is perfectly normal. You get married, you make a home, you have children, they grow up, they get married, you take a mistress. Every respectable French man has a mistress, *Monsieur*. Even *Monsieur* Le President.'

'It is disgusting,' said *Madame* Crochet, 'for a man of his age.'

'But the President is not old,' said *Monsieur* Crochet.

'I was talking about my former husband,' she said.

'And I was talking to *Monsieur* Johnson.'

The Crochets still lived together. They certainly spoke – well at least they shouted – to each other. They could well be sleeping in the same bed and *Monsieur* Crochet had never taken a mistress. The divorce however clearly represented a matter of principle.

'It is not that I ever wanted another woman, *Monsieur*. It is just that now I can, if I change my mind.'

'There is not a woman in the whole of France who would become the mistress of that man,' she said.

'I used to be the most handsome young man in the village,' he said. 'There are those that remember. Why don't you ask the Widow Lambert?'

Madame Crochet made sniffling noises. Then she picked up her knitting and made two stitches.

'That is for the bicycle,' she said.

'Bicycle?' I asked.

'Yes, the one that has just come down the street. Two wheels. Two stitches. A car is four stitches. A lorry is six. This way I know how many vehicles are using our street. For one hour each day I do the count. Not the same hour but one hour. At the end of the month I count the stitches and write down the information for *Monsieur le Maire*. It is important work, *Monsieur*. One day perhaps they will make a new road – a bypass. It is now very dangerous.'

I had always considered the local traffic flow to be insignificant –

114

rush hour was two cars following each other up the village street. From the perspective of someone who had grown up when horse-drawn vehicles were more common than motorised ones it would seem very different.

Our next job was to replace the two front doors – one of which, in what we call the barn, was previously the access to Celestine Toutanu's restaurant bar.

Both doors were big – a metre wide and a metre and a half high. These were not sizes we could pick up from the local *bricolage*. Then, by coincidence I am sure, a double glazing scout arrived.

In France door-to-door selling is highly regulated. Before you agree to a sales visit you set the ground rules. The salesman was to have no more than 45 minutes of our time and we were going to talk doors only – two large ones.

On the appointed day the salesman arrived. It must be that lightweight Italian suits and slip-on suede shoes are the international uniform of door and glazing salesmen

We explained what we wanted – two big oak doors. He consulted charts and tables and tapped figures into his calculator. First one door, then the other, then the sub total, then the sub total plus VAT. Then he wrote down the figure. It was exactly €20,000. We said we'd think about it.

There had to be a cheaper solution. We borrowed a van and set off for *Brico Dépôt* where we found two solid oak doors of the correct size. One opened right and the other left. The total cost was a touch under €1,000. Ricky fitted them both in two days. We were learning.

Perhaps it was the spring sap rising, but I noticed that I had begun to take a particular interest in kissing. Certainly the French *embrassades* – the peck on each cheek – is a custom of which I wholly approve.

A word of warning: the verb 'baiser' is to kiss, but it also means to screw. To confuse matters more, a second verb 'baisser' can mean to drop, go down or lower, whilst its reflexive derivative 'se baisser' is to bend down. There is much embarrassment potential here and the words are best avoided. 'Embrasser' is the safe alternative.

The procedure itself can also become complicated. Take the school crossing patrol for instance. Madame the Lollipop Lady will bend down and kiss every child as they prepare to cross the road. It is so wonderful to watch and great fun. The Health and Safety people in the UK would ban it immediately.

But there are rules – let's call them the pecking protocols. The big questions to be resolved are 'who?', 'where?', 'when?', and 'how often?' I have, for the sake of international relations, researched this.

I began with the principle that the younger and prettier the lady, the more likely it was that the custom would be applied. Not so. As Doris observed of my own pecking preferences at one village function, a particularly attractive middle aged lady received my puckering attentions on four or five occasions. I put this down to my English sense of chivalry; why should it only be the younger ladies who get lucky?

But what does it all amount to? Well, you start by kissing friends, and like many other British expats I have fully embraced this. With the Brits who kisses whom first is not important, but when international puckering is involved it is best to let French friends make the first move.

The number of kisses may also seem arbitrary. Again not so. In most of rural France it is four kisses, in the towns it is either four or three apart from Paris where the norm is two.

The other thing to remember is always start with the left cheek. It is amazing to watch children as young as two proffering the left cheek.

20
One Wedding and
a Bedroom

In early summer we took a Saturday trip to Civray – a market town some 40 kilometres distant. The Charente, a blue snake around Civray, creates a natural boundary and shunts almost all commerce into one compact area. A large park, just beyond the grip of the snake, is the principal recreational area where there is a boating lake, tennis courts and an outdoor swimming pool.

It is a universal truth in France that the pool is the focus of young people's lives on summer days. As we ate our picnic in the park we watched mothers and grandmothers guard towels between taking the occasional cooling dip. Boys chased girls who obligingly slowed down if the boys were not quite fast enough. The lifeguard sat in the shade of the soft drinks stand chatting to two provocatively posed nymphets.

The town centre was empty apart from a handful of venerable shoppers and a couple of lads buzzing around on rusty mopeds.

Around the middle of the afternoon the mood changed as a wedding party gathered outside the *Mairie*. Briefly they all ducked inside for the civil ceremony, then emerged onto the shimmering pavement. The bride, a well-upholstered woman, was compressed into a short off-white dress with matching trainers. She lit a cigarette. A surly youth of around half her age, possibly her son, also lit up. She leaned towards him, first wagging a finger then thrusting her hands on her hips. The youth threw his cigarette into the street and stomped away. She turned, shrugged, sought the groom and gave him a long theatrical kiss. This started a dozen cameras clicking. The bride and groom then framed various passionate poses, one of which had her suspended from his neck with her knees twisted round the back of his thighs. Next, to satisfy the photographers – all of whom were male – she broke away and draped herself over the bonnet of a red sports car. Finally, as another wedding party began to congregate, she shoe-horned herself into the passenger seat.

Within seconds the groom was driving her away as various metal objects tied to the rear bumper clattered on the roadway. The other wedding guests ran to their own cars and followed. They made three circuits of the town centre – the bridal car leading the way. The other guests followed, orchestrating the procession with their horns, at least half of which were illegal – one was a blast of the Can Can and another was a reggae take on the Marseillaise. I wish I had videoed the proceedings as there was enough source material for an anthropological thesis.

By now we had become fed up, even in summer, with sleeping in the close confines of our caravan. We reckoned that moving indoors – albeit still camping out on the sitting room floor – would be an incentive to get on with the required work in the bedroom.

It worked a treat: in just two weeks we stripped off layers of wallpaper, cleaned out and scrubbed all the cupboards, wardrobes, windows and doors, and sanded and stained the floor. Meanwhile Ricky busied himself patching the ceiling around the new beams and plastering over the fireplace that had been removed. Then it was another clean all round before setting to with the emulsion.

On October 13th 2004 we slept in our own bedroom for the first time since May 1st the previous year. Perhaps, of all the stages of renovation, this was the one which made us feel we had really 'moved in'. We celebrated in style by taking cocoa and books to bed.

Photo 16 The *en suite* bedroom is completed

But we were still preparing food in the caravan which meant that everything – including our late night cocoa – had to be transported to the house. When it rained the servings became diluted in transit. Having a proper kitchen with all the appliances installed and functioning was going to be a huge bonus. Fortunately this was achieved, without further misadventure, within a few weeks.

21
Remembrance Day

Everything in France starts or finishes with drinks.

On November 11th we attended the memorial service. This was an entirely civil affair, conducted largely by *Monsieur* Cabacou, the Mayor. The guest of honour was the region's Chief of Police, *Monsieur* Menotte, who also lives in Entrechoux.

As far as I know, in England the ceremony universally takes place at 11.00, but in France there are local variations. In Entrechoux it was set for 11.30, so we decided to have our own little ceremony, with some English friends, before the official one.

Just before 11.00 we marched from our front door the full 20 metres to the war memorial. As the church clock struck the hour we stood with our heads bowed for the two minutes' silence. There are, I suppose, special thoughts for each of us, but for me it is always the friends I lost serving in Malaya.

The minutes between the two ceremonies were just enough for us to pop back to La Maison D'Etre for a cup of tea.

The 'official' ceremony began with the firing of a maroon. The Mayor bent down and lit the match, it went off instantly – a problem with the fuse I think – and seared the skin on his cheek enough to make it bleed. He ignored the wound completely, not even raising a finger to touch it, and stepped back into line.

Everyone faced the solitary memorial. *Monsieur* Cabacou, with natural *gravitas* and a fine fruity voice gave a short address. Then the Deputy Mayor, *Monsieur* St. Nectaire, read the names from the column listing those who had died in two world wars.

After each name, a third man repeated '*mort pour La France*'. It was only after the final '*mort pour La France*' that the two minute silence began.

This simple ceremony was perhaps the biggest culture shock we had experienced since coming to France. The ceremony was, I suppose, similar to those held in thousands of villages in Britain, but there were no uniforms, no medals and no priests. The Republic is a great leveller and that's fine with me.

After the ceremony we retired to the *salle de fête* for drinks.

Of the couple of dozen of us, five were English and one was Dutch. As we are on the fringe of the *Cognac* region we drank *pineau* which is traditionally a mixture of unfermented grape juice and inferior brandy that works pretty well. The 'home brew' versions – made locally from a second pressing of the brandy grapes – are sensational.

We spoke French to the best of our abilities. We even spoke French to the other English as it was somehow the right thing to do on the occasion.

But, as we were about to leave, the Mayor, *Monsieur* Cabacou, detached himself from a group of friends and cut us off at the door.

'*Monsieur, Madame*,' I just want to say how good it is to have our English friends sharing our day of remembrance. Sometimes I think the nations are better friends in war than they are in peace. But I hope you have been made welcome here in Entrechoux.'

Doris assured him that we had been made very welcome. He smiled.

'That is very good,' he said, 'very good. We are, you know a little old fashioned. You will find pies on window ledges that are cooling ... not thawing. And there are still those who believe that the most important thing to have in a modern home is a family.'

'We believe in these things, too,' said Doris.

He smiled again, and inclined his head a little.

'I know that, *Madame*,' he said, 'which is why you are so welcome to our village. May I ask you something?'

'Certainly,' said Doris.

'What do you think of the hunt?'

This question was both unexpected and a potential minefield. Although we are not repulsed by hunting, we basically just don't see the point. Doris said something to that effect.

'I understand,' said *Monsieur* Cabacou, 'but perhaps you will agree that traditionally, in French villages there are three things that govern our lives – the commune, the church, and the hunt. I say 'govern' because we French have a strange attitude to government. In Britain you think politicians are honest until you learn they are not. In France we assume all politicians are corrupt. So, the less they interfere in our lives the better. Less government is best government. And no government in France would ban the hunt. I say this *Monsieur* because we have heard that the hunt is to be banned in England.'

Doris and I had regularly seen able-bodied men (over sixteen) meet after church on Sundays for the purpose of massacring wildlife. The dogs you see are invariably spaniels or retrievers and there are no horses either – just tons of weaponry loaded into white vans. The tradition has been for the men to wear camouflage suits, although it is now accepted that this conceals man from animal less effectively than man from man. The result – a number of fatal accidents – has encouraged the wearing of red vests and hats. This scenario is mirrored throughout rural France. It has little in common with English fox hunting. A few do hunt with horse and hound, but generally the French hunt resembles what we would call 'rough shooting'. It covers almost all types of terrain and social boundaries. What is hunted depends on where you are: rabbits, birds and wild boar are as likely victims as the fox.

'So you are saying that the hunt is to do with freedom?' said Doris.

'More than that, Madame. The chasse represents the personal right of the peasant to take an evening stroll with his dogs for the purpose of catching rabbits. It has not always been so. But, after the revolution, the landowners who survived thought it prudent to share more of what they had with the peasants. Giving permission to hunt on their land was a small price to pay to ensure that their heads remained on their necks. And the hunt was one of the few pleasures not prohibited by the Germans. They knew that for many of us it was the only way of putting something more exotic than cheese on the table. So, at that time, the hunt was also the only legitimate reason for possessing a weapon.'

'But there are accidents,' I said.

'That is true. But then the hunt also represents the freedom to take risks. If you fall off a castle wall it is your own fault. There may even be a notice which tells you it will be your own fault. In the UK I understand you have 4,000 civil servants who make up your Health and Safety Executive. Is it not their job to stop you taking risks? And do you know how many people are employed in the Public Safety Department in France? There are six, Monsieur. What do you think of that?'

'I think perhaps that the French sometimes take too many risks. Look at the deaths on the road.'

Monsieur Cabacou shrugged his shoulders and smiled.

'Risk is in our character, *Monsieur*. If our government tried to tax speeding in the British way there would be another revolution. The words 'Gatso' and 'Gestapo' often appear in the same sentence in French newspapers. Again it is a reminder of the past. Just like today. We cherish the freedoms we fought for in the War. We will not give them away. This is why the French police will not serve speeding notices incurred in the UK on the owners of vehicles registered in France, but on French roads they catch as many as they can. That is fair. That is the true spirit of the hunt.'

Monsieur Cabacou smiled again.

'I must go now,' he said, 'but you know my office hours. You are always welcome to pop in for an argument. I would enjoy that. Although, of course, as your Mayor it is your duty to let me win.'

'I will remember that,' I said.

22
Big Strong Boys

There were still many 'left over' jobs to do, which included fitting the new big window in our bedroom, some smaller windows elsewhere, and building a dais in the sitting room. For further inspiration we made our first visit to Limoges and it was there that we began to realise we were suffering from – *bric* allergy – a kind of hot sweaty sensation that hits you whenever you visit the *bricolage*.

DIY can become addictive, and France reinforces the craving with thousands of *bricolages*, *bricodépôts* and *bricolots*. But you only begin to realise the addiction has you in its grasp when, instead of heading for the guidebook attractions of a great city, your car automatically steers itself to a *bricolage* superstore. You know instinctively where they will be sited – on the city ring road close to McDonald's and the cheap shoes and frocks emporia.

Further symptoms are evidenced by television viewing habits. Others may need a regular fix of Coronation Street. But for us it was '*Big Strong Boys*' that became compulsive viewing, particularly as this was on at 12.30 when everyone in France, apart from the insane (and those who work at McDonald's) stops for lunch.

For the unaddicted let's just say that this is a programme in which two DIY megastars do up houses. A strong feature of the programme is that they show you 'the tricks of the trade'.

There is also an associated website. I opened my server, typed in *'Big Strong Boys'* and what I got was a variety of 'adult' sites with the kind of product offers that varied from the pornographic to the hysterical. Some of the clothing, or perhaps we should say 'accessories', looked uncomfortable enough to endanger the species.

We had by now become active members of an English speaking Christian group – the Chaplaincy of Charente – and through the organisation had met many new friends. I cannot overstate how important joining an organisation of like-minded can be. It helped us both to remain calm and focused at a time when we might otherwise have begun to question the wisdom of the move. The experience of the other members of the Chaplaincy was like a beacon of light; whatever happened to us had happened to somebody else, so there were shared insights, experiences and solutions. There was also a new network of contacts and friends. We attend a 'home group' each week.

The 'home group' idea works well in the Charente; there are ten inter-linked groups of eight or more people. The cornerstone of the Chaplaincy is Christian fellowship, but this also manifests itself in a number of practical ways – such as swapping information on matters such as law, taxes, medical matters and even cheap ferry crossings. The group is also a forum for DIY advice and the practical exchange of skills and experience. I only wish I had joined from the very beginning.

The meetings invariably begin with tea, coffee and cake and then we join together in songs of praise. My job is to play guitar and lead the singing. Part of my belief is that God is neither a snob nor a music critic.

After the singing we have a discussion or bible study. The atmosphere is light and reflective. Ultimately, the religious nature of the meetings is set aside and the session becomes informal.

One of the major topics of conversation with Chaplaincy friends is, 'Do you like it out here?', 'Would you go back to England?'

Whilst nobody likes to admit the French adventure has been a disaster, it is equally clear that some have made a greater success of it than others. By the Autumn of 2004, the rise in UK property values during the previous year meant that bridges were smouldering; we had already recognised that ours were completely conflagrated. Although property values had also risen in the Charente during the same period (by up to 40%) that increase started from a lower price base. We had also by now invested far more of our capital than intended in the property.

But there were unexpected compensations. The biggest tug towards England is the family and this feeling, certainly shared by many of our Chaplaincy friends, must be a major factor in how well people settle. It is all very well saying to yourself that England is just a thin strip of water away, but in emotional terms it can feel like a million miles.

But then again how many people have family and friends two miles away and never see them? How many people buy a home with three extra bedrooms for all the people who say they will visit, but never turn up? Certainly we are aware of those in both categories.

It was already clear that things would be different for us. Bearing in mind that the property was still only barely equipped to receive visitors we had already had so many that the restoration process had fallen further behind. Of course that had at least something to do with 13 grandchildren at the latest count – eight of whom are under eight years of age, but we had also been tracked down by many friends.

We came to the conclusion that part of the reason for the continuous family invasion is the attraction of France itself. Let's face it, doesn't 'visiting family in the Charente' sound so much better than 'visiting family in Essex'? Case proven.

23
The Peasant Economy

Around half the workforce in France is on the minimum wage. One consequence of this, and something we had already realised was another plus on the balance sheet of French rural life, was the peasant economy.

One evening in October, just as it was going dark, I opened the door to a man selling apples.

'*Vous voulez des pommes, Monsieur?*'

I thought a couple of kilos would come in handy and said so.

'*Non, Monsieur, ce n'est pas possible. Cinquante kilos minimum.*'

And that's the way it works, be it fish, fowl or just about anything that happens to be in season. Or, in the immortal words of John Sullivan: 'no income tax, no VAT ...'

The peasant economy is as much an institution as the hunt. It also begins to explain why local fresh food (and the French place a premium on 'local') is relatively expensive in supermarkets. It is simply because the French believe it makes more sense to sell local produce locally than see it transported along the *autoroute* network.

Another compensation was beginning to filter through on the bills front. Our local taxes for the first year were going to amount to around £300 – a quarter of our previous council tax bill in Kent. As electricity is still cheaper than in the UK, the meter seemed to stroll rather than race which, no doubt, also had much to do with living outside. We expected to be harder hit by the winter quarter, but the log burning stove was already beginning to prove its worth.

Perhaps the greatest compensation was living amongst the French themselves. They have a genuinely high regard for intellect and education. They talk knowledgeably about nuances of debate in politics and religion. They are at the same time gregarious, yet have a dislike of too much formal or organised activity. These kinds of apparent contradiction make them elusive, infuriating, introverted, intriguing, beguiling, and most frequently, charming. Best of all, the children are respectful and well-mannered which bodes well for the future.

It is worth noting that when responding to questions about their motivation for buying property in France, the British are inclined to list priorities which include cost, climate and cuisine. All that, to a greater or lesser extent, may be true, but I have no doubt that the British may receive a more positive response, and give themselves a much better chance of settling in, if they placed the French themselves towards the top of the list.

24
Walls, Windows and Doors

Doris was in charge of renovating the interior stonework. Charente limestone looks good and cleans up well.

She uses a product called 'Enduit de Parement Restauration' – which translates literally as 'Coating of Restoration Adornment'. The product is available in a kaleidoscope of shades – each subtly different. So, as with other adornments – such as wallpaper, hair colour and car touch-up paint – it is vital to remember the product number.

Doris had her own working method. First she took out just enough mortar to show off the natural shape of stones; she found an old screwdriver best for this. When she had finished picking out a section, she attacked the wall with a sturdy, stiff brush. Then she made a thickish mix of proprietary-branded grout (the traditional formula is sand and lime) and pushed it into the gaps using her fingers. Some people trowel it on from a float while others throw the mix at the wall and wipe off the excess. Whatever method is preferred it is essential to wear rubber gloves because of the lime. When the grout was almost dry Doris brushed again with a stiff brush, this removed the excess which was then remixed and reused.

After that it basically depends on the stone. I have seen a silicone coating – painted or even sprayed on – used effectively. It protects the stone and gives a soft sheen finish. We thought the stone work looked just fine as it was so we left it '*au naturel*'.

We had hoped to restore the two large windows in the living room, but close inspection confirmed that they were too far gone, which meant new frames and glass. The glass was traditional two millimetre but the now more common four millimetre offers much better insulation. You can, in theory, put four millimetre in an old frame, but it's tricky as there's not much gap for the putty. We decided to do it properly putting the better quality glass into new frames.

Photo 17 The completed living room

Ricky came to the rescue. Someone else he was working for had a couple going spare and they were brand new. The man had travelled 100 miles to Poitiers to get them and had already treated them with ten year varnish. They looked wonderful. The only snag was that they didn't fit, and, as he had already coated them with ten year varnish, he couldn't take them back.

Ricky measured them and was confident they would do for us. I offered the purchase price less 20% and this was accepted.

The only problem was that Doris had already decorated the room. The last thing we wanted was the mess of fitting new windows. Again Ricky came through, fitting them in two days with barely a scratch. We felt that our luck was changing.

The next job was to get rid of the old back door and replace it. Doris had set her heart on a stable door arrangement. Again Ricky felt he was up to the job.

'You price up the wood,' he said, 'I don't think it will be very expensive. Then I'll sort out the job. I reckon it will cost you a couple of days' wages.'

Again he was 100% right. In fact it worked out even better than that. The wood was cheap, the job was perfect and the new door made a huge difference to the appearance of the back of the house.

Our rear barn doors were on their last legs. They had not been a priority. I reckoned that as they had done the job for 150 years or so they could last a little longer, but now the back of the house looked tidy, they stood out – no longer shabby chic, just knackered. They sagged and swayed and there were gaps in the planking that let in enough cold air to freeze the pipes in winter.

I had considered the problem for months. Openings for doors and windows made from huge hand sawn blocks of Charente limestone are usually true, but when I measured the barn openings nothing was remotely so. I decided the first thing to do was to put a straight strip of concrete across the floor of the opening and work up from there.

Once the openings were true I started with the 'small' door first. I made a frame from 4 x 5 inch pine and filled this in with two centimetre tongue and groove floor boarding. As the door was two metres high by a metre and a half wide, I knew that when the bracing battens were added, it was going to be heavy.

Photo 18 The barn door, before and after

Doris had gone to England to welcome another grandchild into the world and, with Ricky employed elsewhere, I was on my own. The door was ready but horizontal and I had made and fitted a rebated frame. The problem was how to lift the door to the frame.

I considered a cry for help to one of our local friends but my stubbornness got in the way. There had to be a way. It took a while before I came up with the solution – the wheelbarrow.

I managed to get the new door on to it without injury. The problem now was that – as I could not see over the door – I was travelling blind. I turned a little at a time – feeling round the edge of the frame to check my course. When I was confident I was in position I tipped the door out of the barrow roughly into position. Then with a shove or three I wedged it into place and completed the job by fitting the hinges. It was now simply a matter of doing the same thing with the other, larger, doors.

When Doris came home I could not contain the triumphant tone in my voice.

'What do you think?' I said.

'Wonderful,' she said, 'but I see that you've left me the job of staining the wood.'

Ricky left us in June as there was not much for him to do now and he was keen to start his new business.

The last job he did was making and fitting a window in the big bedroom. Again it was first class workmanship. I made a new inside sill and Doris fitted some drapes.

'We're going to miss Ricky,' said Doris.

'Well, he did suggest that you visit him soon,' I said.

'To help him set up the business?'

'No, he's got all the help he needs. He was thinking that you might be a customer. A gesture of appreciation for all he has done. And he said you wouldn't have to have a particularly large tattoo ...'

25
Charente Christmas

Christmas 2004 was to be our first in France.

'I would like to make a special day of it,' said Doris.

'Then let's ring round a few people and see what can be arranged,' I said.

It worked out there were going to be nine of us for Christmas dinner so we felt that, rather than heaping the responsibility on one family, we would arrange a meal out. We came up with a list of restaurants to try. Nine people, 12.30, Christmas Day. Simple.

Not one of them was open. We extended our list and tried again. Nothing. We went back to our friends and asked for their recommendations. Another list. Another failure. Finally, somebody came up with another possible.

'It's not the best, David. To be honest it's not even the tenth best but it's always open. What do you think?'

'I think we're getting desperate,' I said, 'I'll give them a call.'

The setting of the restaurant was lovely. The food was not. And there was no special Christmas menu, but the day was sunny and bright and we enjoyed sitting by the bank of the Charente, and with good cheer and good company it did at least feel like Christmas.

I have since found out the reason why French eateries do not open for Christmas lunch; French Christmas celebrations start with a festive meal on Christmas Eve and go on well into the night. Consequently, many people are on to the hair of the dog, raw egg yolks or Epsom salts by Christmas lunchtime.

On January 1st 2005 I encountered *Monsieur* Crochet tapping his way down the street. Despite his age and disability he is hugely independent. Nevertheless, with more than a touch of frost on the pavement, I was surprised to find him out alone.

'She has gone to her sister's house in Limoges,' he explained, 'but it is only for one week.'

'Is this for a New Year celebration?' I asked.

'I do not think so, *Monsieur*, she does not like her sister. They fight like cats.'

'Well,' I said, 'it is perhaps a good thing. And anyway you need someone to look after you.'

He shook his head as if unable to take this in.

'But *Monsieur*,' he said, 'did you not know? I have the Widow Lambert to look after me. The arrangement is, shall we say, satisfactory. I am hoping that my former wife will make peace with her sister. Then perhaps she will make many visits to Limoges. *Bonne Année*.'

26
The 70th Celebration

The next job was fitting and tiling the *en suite* bathroom and I wasn't sure I was up to it.

'The trouble is,' said Doris, 'that Ricky was too competent. But we've learnt so much. I'm sure we'll get it right.'

I was less certain. My last tiling experience had been 40 years earlier and I recalled that I'd made a mess of it. The best thing perhaps was to try something else first, something simple. I made a frame and boxed in the bath. So far so good.

As the shower cubicle and tray were already in place I had run out of room for procrastination. I mentioned this to a friend at the Chaplaincy.

'I've done some tiling,' he said, 'would you like a bit of help?'

'More than a bit,' I said.

'Then you shall have it,' he said.

It was now the end of June and Doris was busily planning for my 70th birthday in July. We were expecting perhaps two dozen of our immediate family to come out for the big day.

The problem was sleeping accommodation. We had done our calculations and even with a couple of tents for the older children and using the living area as emergency bed space, we were still struggling.

'It's a pity there are no vampires in the family,' I said, 'they would be comfortable hanging from the rafters in the barn.'

'Not with the amount that our lot can drink,' said Doris, 'they'd fall off.'

We considered our options; we had friends who could put people up nearby or we could book some of the family into a local hotel. Neither of these ideas was the answer. Apart from the family politics involved, it cut across the idea of having the whole family together for as long as possible. One of my sons was coming in his motor home so that would help, but even with extending the tent city to all the children, we were still a couple of bed spaces short. The only solution was to put the old caravan back into service.

In fact the van had remained in occasional use. It was ideal for sleeping when the weather was hot because it cooled down more quickly than the house after dusk. Hooked up to the electric, and with its 'en suite' shower and toilet, it was perfect for a couple. However, for safety as well as aesthetic reasons it needed securing on a permanent base. It is something I should have done earlier, but having become an expert in putting down concrete I was now confident that I could take it on.

The first job is to work out how much concrete you need. Most DIY books will have charts showing how much is required for a given area and depth but, in general, you need about four inches of concrete laid over a bed of hardcore. The actual depth depends on the surface you are working on; soft soil needs more hardcore than hard.

I did not need to be too precise as I was mixing my own concrete and I knew there would be other jobs I could do using the same materials. It was just a case of making sure that I had enough, and anyway our local builders' yard delivers any quantity for €20.

At the yard I ordered three tons of sand and gravel mixed (ballast), two tons of sand and eight bags of cement. The girl complimented me on my French, I was delighted, not because my French was truly wonderful, but because it proved I now had complete confidence in doing my own ordering.

The next thing was to find a cement mixer. I knew our new English neighbour, Derek, had one. Better still, it turned out that he was not only prepared to let me use it but he offered to come along and help.

Derek, Doris and I worked together. Derek mixed, Doris was on barrow duties, and I laid it down. Initially we mixed it too dry, then settled on nine shovels of ballast to six of sand and one battered washing up bowl of cement. Perfect. I put down the mix over an old iron bed frame – also provided by Derek.

Photo 19 Doris mixing cement

It took the three of us four days. This was largely because rain kept stopping play, but the job was finished – and I think pretty well done in the circumstances. I now had a full 24 hours to spare to move the caravan onto its new hard standing before the birthday guests arrived.

On the day of the big celebration I woke up to blazing sunshine and a house full of family and friends. It was just wonderful. OK, so I was officially old now, but my mood was geriatrically blissful, so blissful in fact that when I opened the letter from the British department of work and pensions, I felt only mildly homicidal.

'We stopped paying your pension a year ago,' they advised me, *'and you have no right of appeal.'*

Doris poured me a strong dose of anti-panic tea. Fortified by this I rang Newcastle where I was informed by a bubbly female that my pension had been stopped because I had not returned their *'Life Certificate'* – basically a declaration that I had not yet been nailed down in my little wooden box.

I explained that there was a logical reason for this: despite the fact that they, self-evidently, had my new address I had not received the appropriate form.

'Don't worry,' she said, 'I'll send you another one. It happens all the time.'

'Not to me,' I said, 'And anyway, you attached one with the letter I have in front of me. It tells me that, as I hadn't previously filled in the form, I previously didn't get, I'm as dead as mutton with no right of appeal.'

'Don't worry,' she said, 'just fill in the form and send it back. We'll reinstate your pension immediately.'

So I filled in the form and sent it off as a registered letter.

It might seem strange that I did not know that my pension had been stopped for a year. The oversight occurred because our pensions are paid into our English accounts in pounds sterling. We could have asked for payment in euros, but may have lost out to the constantly fluctuating exchange rate. What we try to do is leave the sterling in the account and only convert to euros having tracked the rate to a moment that seems advantageous.

I follow the rate movements through satellite TV, or for an instant update I press the red button on my Sky remote whilst tuned to BBC 1. Then I toggle through the menu to Foreign Exchange and go to the Bank of England pound/euro rate. This sets the benchmark for contacting a foreign currency dealer to find who comes closest to the Bank of England rate.

After a while you get the instinct for the best time to buy. Obviously there are no guarantees, but it does at least give you more control over your money. I cannot be the only one doing it as there are plenty of ads for currency dealers in French lifestyle magazines.

Of course, to get a really good deal, you need to exchange a decent wad. We tend to do it in £10,000 blocks, which you can live on for quite a long time in France. This also explains why I had no idea that I had been dead for a year. Given the circumstances I felt remarkably well and, in due course, after another phone call or two, they reinstated my pension and paid the arrears up to date.

27
Fireworks and Snails

A few days after my birthday we went to a firework display in Paroisse. The French love their '*feu d'artifice*' and my experience is that the displays are either good or very good. This one, set off by the old castle keep, was superb, so much so that not many of us in the crowd noticed the onset of unseasonable rain.

During a lull in the entertainment I felt a hand on my shoulder.

'Remember *Monsieur*, always to run downhill,' said the owner of the hand.

It was old Maurice of the hunt.

'I never walk in the woods without remembering that,' I said.

He laughed vigorously and shook my hand.

'But we are quite safe here *Monsieur*,' he said, '*the feu d'artifice* will keep the bears away.'

'I am glad to hear it,' I said, 'I imagine that they don't like the noise.'

'Just so, *Monsieur*.'

Conversation was rendered temporarily impossible by a succession of impressive bangs, but the old man remained by my side. Between the crackles and crashes of the display, I believe I could hear the cogs in his brain whirring. During a brief truce in the battle to illuminate the sky he put his hand back on my shoulder. It was my cue to pay attention.

'You know,' he said slowly, 'I have something to tell you. About your house.'

I nodded as a starburst explosion went off over our heads.

'You will know that the property was once a restaurant. Not a good restaurant but not always bad. Much depended on the mood of *la proprietaire*.'

'*Madame* Toutanu?'

'Well, yes and no. It was the mood of Basil, *Monsieur* Toutanu, that was important. He was the *chef de cuisine*. But when *Madame* was not happy *Monsieur* was not happy. You understand?'

Again I nodded as the sky was lit with glittering red and gold.

'And you knew when *Monsieur* Basil was unhappy. He would refuse to go to the kitchen. He would refuse to talk. He would just sit in silence at the small table by the window.'

'On his own?'

'Sometimes, *Monsieur*. But most frequently he would play chequers.'

'With a friend?'

'No *Monsieur*, because that would have required him to talk. No, he played with *Monsieur* Méchant, his dog, who was what you call a *Setter Irlandais*.'

'An Irish Setter, playing chequers?'

'It was most curious and unusual, *Monsieur* Méchant, who was very large, would sit on the floor at the opposite side the small table to *Monsieur* Basil. He would wait his turn. He would think. Then he would push the chequers with his nose.'

'He must have been a very intelligent dog,' I observed.

'I don't think so, *Monsieur*. I once saw him lose three games in a row.'

Maurice gripped me by the shoulder again, as he walked away, I could still hear him laughing.

We stayed to the end of the firework display before heading for home, moist but mellow.

Driving on twisting country lanes late at night in France is like it was in parts of rural England forty years ago. You can go for miles and see nobody and, when the moon is obscured by cloud it is dark, very dark.

Suddenly up ahead there were faint pulses of light that turned to a twinkling as we came close. And there, by the hedgerow, was a family – Mum, Dad, three children and a dog. All had supermarket bags and torches, except the dog who had a special green flashing collar. They were collecting *escargots*.

We had seen this many times before, invariably after a shower or two, but never this late at night. The vision had a Stephen King quality to it.

I asked our neighbour, Bernard, about this.

'I am sorry, *Monsieur*, if the English do not like *l'escargots*.'

And that is the reaction I always get. It is a kind of apology and accusation at the same time.

The method is this. First catch the snails and put them in

supermarket bags, next carry them home and put them in special cages for a month with a diet of nothing but white flour.

'The *escargots*,' *Monsieur*, 'are used to this,' Bernard confided.

Anyway, after the month of flour you take them out of their shells and cut off the tail part – which contains the liver.

Then, whilst the shells are cleaning up nicely in a bowl of tepid water, you cook the snails themselves in something hotter, the snails are then put back in their shells ready for serving. I imagine each shell and snail has to be marked so that the match up works as it should.

The debate, of course, is in the cooking method. Our friend Natalie *sautés* them in white wine, while Bernard favours a sauce made from butter, parsley and garlic. The regional recipe – for *escargots Charentaise* – has them lightly fried in oil, with garlic and onion, before serving them with spicy potatoes and a Bolognaise style sauce. Delicious, I am sure.

Photo 20 David in his upstairs office

28
A Most Secret History

It was a near perfect summer day as it often is in the Charente, not too hot, just a faint flow of breeze. I was sitting in the garden near the stream with my book. The sound of the water over the stones may have made me drowsy, because at first I did not recognise my visitor.

But there was perhaps a better excuse for that. Celestine Toutanu was almost entirely reinvented. Gone were the dowdy shawl and clumpy shoes; the woman before me was a ringer for Bette Davis in *'Whatever Happened to Baby Jane'*. The hair had changed from grey to strawberry blonde, the lipstick and shoes were holly berry red.

'*Madame*,' I said, 'it is a delight to see you again.'

'Your wife, *Madame* Johnson, also said you would be *électrisier*.'

'Thrilled?'

'That also, *Monsieur*.'

I found her a plastic chair.

'Have you been offered some refreshment?' I asked.

'*Madame* Johnson is finding something profitable *pour la gorge*.'

'I am afraid we have no *absinthe*.'

'A good thing, *Monsieur*. It makes me break the wind. Like the owl, remember? No, *Madame* Johnson is looking for the park.'

'The park?'

'The park of the high land?

'Oh, yes. Highland Park whisky. *Très profitable*. It comes from Orkney.'

'I think it comes from a bottle *Monsieur*.'

Doris arrived with a tray featuring, amongst the peripherals, a large pot of tea and a bottle of whisky. Celestine glanced at the bottle and nodded as if to claim her small success in determining the origin of the whisky. Doris poured her a large one.

'So what brings you to Entrechoux, *Madame*?'

'It was the bus *Monsieur*. But I am here to see 'Le Petit Chateau'. And, of course, my favourite English peoples.'

Celestine sipped her whisky and looked around the garden. She complimented us on the work we had done and sipped a little more. Then, little by little and whisky by whisky she steered the conversation towards the past. Finally, when we had reached the Second World War she began to sob, gently at first, and then with gusto. We were becoming concerned.

'It does not matter, *Madame*,' Doris said, 'you do not have to talk about it.'

Celestine wiped her eyes on a pink handkerchief, composed herself, and sat very upright.

'But I want to tell you,' she said.

We waited whilst the handkerchief was returned to a pocket.

147

'As you know,' she said, 'there were Germans living in 'Le Petit Chateau'. One of them, the *Capitaine*, was very handsome. His name was Jurgen. Although, the house was the *propriété* of my family, I was employed there as *une femme de chambre*. 'Chamber maid?'

'Yes *Monsieur*. He gave me gifts. Some were quite *précieux*. Precious. And, in time we became lovers. I do not regret that *Monsieur*. It gave me a penis.'

There was a brief double take. Then I realised what she meant to say.

'Happiness?'

'That also, *Monsieur*. But there was a *problème*. In the village they talk. They say I am *une prostituée*. And worse. When it came time for Jurgen to leave, the situation was *très dangereux*. What could we do? I was sent to the house of my uncle. To be, as you say, out of the way. And then they make the fire. To leave the house with no fire would have said to everyone that Celestine is truly the whore of the *Capitaine*. The fire saved my reputation, *Monsieur*, and perhaps my life. The fire said that the *Capitaine* was not my lover. You do not burn the house of your lover, do you *Monsieur*?'

29
Old Friends and New

One of the great things about moving towards the end of renovation is that there is a little more time to enjoy the property.

I used to think that we had just one tree, we nearly decided to cut it down, but changed our minds. I am glad we did. This modest specimen of cherry at the back of the house is just enough to provide picnic and reading shade.

In fact we have a whole row of mature trees along the riverside. I had taken these so much for granted that they were almost invisible, but they were rediscovered, if you like, by Donald the Druid.

Donald is an old friend from our Northumbrian days. He is a free spirit that materialises, causes no hassle, and disappears a few days later. Although he is laid back about everything, he is almost passionate about trees. Happily his passion is also his pleasure; he runs an outdoor centre in the middle of a forest.

Whenever he visits, summer or winter, he sits by the riverside amongst the trees. When I have time to join him, he argues his beliefs and I mine.

Donald is very big on 'permaculture' – sustainable living. He sends us magazines on living cheaply and well off the land. His ideas somehow seem entirely uncontroversial in this quiet corner of

France. The people here are still closer to natural produce than waxed fruit, but of course Donald means much more than that. Whenever he leaves, I feel slightly ashamed. I have a decent plot of land and do little with it, but in time I hope that will be remedied.

We also have some Dutch friends with young children who are setting up a goat farm. Dad is a fair-haired giant who wears the biggest clogs I have ever seen – bright yellow boats which click their course across the cobbles. His plan is to make cheese with hopefully sufficient commercial success to sustain the family. I wish him well.

There is no doubt that the Charente attracts people looking for a simple life. Many of the expats around Entrechoux have chosen to escape not only high pressure jobs but the culture of 'must have' that goes with it. Personalised registrations – or cherished numbers as they call them in the UK – are here referred to as 'vanity plates'. People put their real lives, and those of their neighbours, before 'reality television'. Children play hide and seek round the houses, *boules* on the gravel tracks and chasing games round the village green. Christmas remains, even for the uncommitted, a Christian festival. It is like putting the clock back a couple of generations.

30
Future Plans

It was in July 2005, whilst collecting some items from the *bricolage*, when I found a familiar hand on my shoulder. It belonged to Maurice of the hunt.

'I trust you are well,' I said.

'Very well,' he replied.

'You know,' I said, 'I learned recently that your family had lived in Entrechoux for many years.'

Maurice threw back his shoulders and smiled.

'From the time of François 1st,' he said, 'or maybe earlier.'

'Yes, I was doing some research on my property when I think I found one of your ancestors.'

'Research?'

'Yes, *les archives*.'

'Ah, the archive, at Paroisse sur Charente?'

'That is correct. It seems that *Monsieur* Jacques Bertrand, of Entrechoux, was a great inventor. Your ancestor, I think?'

'As I said, there have been many Bertrands in Entrechoux,

Monsieur. I think at one time half the village were Bertrands. Or married to them. Or sleeping with them. I do not know of *Monsieur* Jacques, but it must be that he was one of us. What was it that he made?'

'He invented the Mouse Trap Charentaise. Very ingenious.'

'Ingenious?'

'Yes, *Monsieur*. It required an understanding of the way the mouse thinks.'

'And how is that?'

'The trap was a simple block of wood. At the centre was a sharp blade. And, at one side of the blade was the bait – a piece of cheese, I think. The mouse scented the bait, climbed on the block, and as he looked over the blade he cut his own head off.'

Maurice shook his head, I could see that his thinking was in overdrive.

'But *Monsieur*,' he said, 'what if he climbed up the other side of the block and simply ran away with the cheese?'

'Ah, but *Monsieur* Jacques Bertrand really did understand mouse psychology. He would allow the creature to be lucky maybe one or two times. Then he had him.'

I knew also that I nearly had Maurice. He rocked his head gently from one shoulder to the other.

'You must explain, *Monsieur*.'

'Ah well, it is like this. At first the mouse has taken the cheese and run away. But this time your ancestor has baited the trap with no cheese.'

Yes my trap was well baited now.

'No cheese?'

'Yes, you see the mouse comes to the block from either direction. He climbs up and cautiously looks over the blade. Then, shaking his head vigorously, he says, '*Merde*, where has the lump of cheese gone?' And that, of course, is fatal, *Monsieur*.'

Maurice paused for a moment, laughed heartily, and shook me by the hand.

'I did not know I had such a genius for an ancestor. I thank you, *Monsieur*.'

We still have plans for further renovation. The downstairs bathroom still needs work and we feel that the barn – valuable store that it was – should have a greater purpose in life. It was large enough, according to one friend, to become a nightclub with a dance floor and bar below and with sound equipment and perhaps exotic dancers' poles in the hayloft or, perhaps I should say, the mezzanine. I have spoken to *Monsieur* Cabacou about this, and once he was sure that I was not entirely serious, he agreed that thumping bass speakers, late night revellers and lunatic drunken driving was exactly what the village needed.

'Very much in keeping with the traditions of Entrechoux,' he said, 'we miss out far too much on the experience of the outside world *Monsieur*. You put your plans in writing, *Monsieur*. I would like to see the expressions on the face of the planning committee.'

More seriously we have considered the idea of developing the barn as a *gîte*, or as bed and breakfast accommodation, or even as a cyclists' hostel – with clean, though fairly primitive, accommodation. I am not sure we will ever do any of these things. There comes a time in life when you don't really want to be taking on long-term commitments.

I have also thought about a terrace. When I get really old I may

153

enjoy a padded lounger in the shade with a suitable light rigged above my head so I can finish my book when the sun goes down.

Planning permission is not required for a terrace unless you go for something larger than 20 square metres or you intend to raise it more than 60 centimetres above ground level. I asked *Monsieur* Cabacou about this and he said that a *déclaration à travaux* (to the *Mairie*) was still required because the terrace adds to the *surface hors d'oeuvre brut* (SHOB) – the official gross floor area of the property also known as the '*surface habitable*'. This could, theoretically, impact on future building plans and increase local taxes, although both scenarios are unlikely.

I have worked out what is required – excavation, levelling, then hardcore covered with coarse sand. This is then topped off with my old friend – reinforced concrete. There should be expansion joints every two metres and a slight slope on the slab – around 2% is enough – for rainwater to drain. It would be cheaper to use *géotextile* material under the sand or wooden frame on concrete, but these, to my mind, may be a short term gain. The weeds come back to get you – eventually.

Decking is now quite popular in France. You can get interlocking panels, pre-drilled boards, and a system they call *caillebotis*– a kind of all weather parquet suspended on height-adjustable pillars. Surprisingly all these systems are considered to be cheaper than putting down a stone surface but, of course, that depends on what you pay for your stone. I am again on the look-out for a suitable load.

Our next big project could well be to replace the Colditz-style chain-link husky fence with a timber structure that provides more privacy. The idea then would be to have a gateway to the stream where we could have a summer house, but these plans have so far been thwarted. They won't let me have a summer house close to the water's edge. The argument is that if we have enough serious rain causing a flood, Doris and I could sail away, Noah-like, for forty days or thereabouts. I am going to have to give this further thought.

But the greatest challenge will always be to make the most of our lives. We came to France for a better life, but we will never be French. We will always be the Brits who live in the mini-chateau by the bridge. That is not an insult. It's a matter of fact.

We left behind our British culture because, apart from real ale and fish and chips, it had pretty much ceased to exist. There are problems in France certainly, but the continuing sense of community and respect for people and property makes it much more like the Britain we grew up in. We do not have to lock our doors in Entrechoux. How many English villages are there where you can still say that?

Photo 21 La Maison D'Etre from the rear

The commonest phrase of criticism you hear from our neighbours is: 'Ce n'est pas normal'. I have always taken this to mean 'It's not quite right'. It can describe just about anything from riots on the streets of Paris to an overcooked piece of pork. It explains all you need to know about the French philosophy of life. There is not much that is bad enough to let it ruin your day. And in that sense at least I think, three years down the line, Doris and I are becoming a little more like the French. And that, we sincerely believe, is something to aspire to.

155

31
Make a Wish

At the end of August 2005 one of my lovely grandchildren, nine year old Simona, made her second visit to La Maison D'Etre. She is every bit as bright as a button.

Behind the house there is a leafy lane that runs down to a river ford. This is a cool area in which the commune has created a picnic area with rough tables and large ornamental boulders.

As we approached this spot I turned away from Simona, cupped my mouth and put on a funny voice.

'I hear tell that she who makes a wish at the water's edge will have it come true.'

She turned to me and smiled.

'You said that last year, Granddad.'

'And did you make a wish?'

'Yes, I did.'

'And did it come true?'

'No,' she said, 'it didn't.'

She hunched her shoulders and shook her head, Then, after brushing away some leaves, she sat on the top of a picnic table.

Then she looked at me curiously.

'Did you make a wish, Granddad?'

'Yes, I did,'

'And did it come true?'

I hesitated for a moment but her eyes demanded an answer.

'Yes poppet,' I said, 'I rather think that it did.'

Photo 22 La Maison D'Etre

Part II
The Practicalities

HOW MUCH DOES IT COST?

RENOVATION PROJECT ESTIMATES

The figures below are necessarily estimates because no two restoration projects are ever the same. At best, or worst, you could be looking at half or double the amounts quoted. These do not include VAT or decoration costs but do assume that all surfaces are appropriately finished.

To renovate a semi-derelict property to a quality standard suitable for short term letting (a *gîte*) or as a bed and breakfast business: between €1,100 and €2,000 per square metre.

To renovate a semi-derelict property to a standard suitable for domestic living: between €780 and €1,800 per square metre.

To renovate a shell property (roof, doors, windows and walls) to a standard suitable for short term letting (a *gîte*) or as a bed and breakfast business: between €1,350 and €2,450 per square metre.

To renovate a shell property (roof, doors, windows and walls) to a standard suitable for domestic living: between €1,230 and €2,250 per square metre.

To renovate and update a recently occupied property, without roof work, to a standard suitable for domestic living: between €550 and €1,060 per square metre.

To renovate and update a recently occupied property, including roof work, to a standard suitable for domestic living: between €650 and €1,350 per square metre.

PART PROJECT ESTIMATES

To rewire a three- to four-bedroom property: approximately €6,850.

To replace a plain, two-pitched roof and to remove old roofing: approximately €100 per square metre.

To replace a two-pitched roof with roof lights and/or dormer windows: approximately €155 per square metre.

To take up an old concrete floor and to replace, including reinforcement and damp courses: approximately €80 per square metre.

To install a septic tank and soak away suitable for a three- to four-bedroomed property: approximately €5,500.

To install a medium-sized window in a stone surround including knocking through and making good: approximately €800.

To install a doorway in a stone surround including knocking through, framing and making good: approximately €1,950.

To remove decayed lime render from walls and to renew with the same. The cost to include specialist equipment hire including scaffolding: approximately €70 per square metre.

To repoint a wall, including necessary preparation and specialist equipment hire including scaffolding: approximately €60 per square metre.

To install an electric hot water tank system suitable for a three- to four-bedroomed property with a kitchen and two bathrooms (or wet rooms): approximately €800.

To install a basic bathroom suite within a floor area of three by two metres, including an over-bath shower, connections, tile surrounds and flooring: approximately €2,000.

To install an unheated and unroofed, freshwater swimming pool with a surface area of ten metres by six metres, including paved surround: approximately €24,500. (Seawater versions cost a similar amount but running costs are reduced.)

To connect to an existing gas supply within 35 metres of the property: approximately €900.

UTILITIES AND SERVICES

ELECTRICITY

The French 220 volt/50 hertz supply is comparable to that of the UK and it is almost exclusively supplied by Électricité de France (EDF). French electricity is still possibly the cheapest in Europe and standards of installation, particularly for new property, are satisfactory.

There are problems with older buildings as some still use the 110/120 volt AC supply which requires a transformer to convert the supply to 220 volts AC for motorised appliances. If the wattage available from the transformer is less than the rating of the appliances, they will not work – or at least not at the same time. More bizarrely the level of supply, even for 220 volts AC, will depend on the KW supply you have metered. This agreed supply level, which can vary from 3 KW to 36 KW, is a significant part of the standing charge equation with the maximum supply costing more than 40% more than the minimum. Small- to medium-size households usually operate on a 6 KW supply with a device known as a *délesteur* – which cuts out 'supplementary systems' (such as convectors and water heaters) when high-consumption appliances (such as washing machines and electric kettles) threaten to overload the system.

Older rural properties may not have an electricity supply and paying to have it connected to the grid can be prohibitively expensive. This is particularly true if the property is within a national park where only underground supplies are permitted. EDF will quote for the work but alternatives, including generators and solar energy, may be more viable.

Even where 220V AC is supplied, rural areas in particular suffer regular power cuts. This is most likely to be a result of a generation or system failure, but could also be a consequence of industrial action. Happily most interruptions are only momentary, but are sufficient to knock out timing devices and to crash computers. Specification for computer systems in France therefore invariably includes an uninterrupted power supply (UPS) with battery backup.

The price for electricity depends on the tariff option you choose. Leaflets explaining the alternatives are issued when each new installation is made and when a new customer account is opened. They are also available on demand from any office of Électricité de France (EDF) and on the internet at www.edf.fr.

They amount to either:

- The Blue Tariff. This is either the normal tariff (*option base*) where charges remain constant throughout the 24-hour cycle, or the reduced rate (*option heures creuses*) where up to three periods (totalling a maximum eight hours a day) are earmarked for lower cost supply. The *option base* is selected by owners of properties that are only occasionally occupied. The reduced rate option, which features a two dial meter which records both 'normal' and 'off peak' usage, is the rate most commonly applied.

- The Tempo Tariff (*option tempo*). This increasingly popular tariff is designed to encourage fuel saving at times when demand is at its greatest. It provides the customer with cheap off-peak electricity for most of the year. There are, however, some variations from this – the most significant being some 22 peak days (falling between 1st November and 31st March) which are determined (by EDF) by reference to the meteorological centre in Toulouse. At these peak periods the tariff charged is up to eight times the off-peak period. Peak days are announced by a light or buzzer. The tempo tariff, which also has a lower standing charge, can only be applied to homes where the power supply is rated at nine or more KW, but there must also be a viable alternative (non-electrical) source of heat. Those who choose the tempo tariff normally have a remote controller which switches off high consumption appliances during the peak periods. This tariff is particularly suitable for people who have a property which is unoccupied during the winter or for those with homes on the Mediterranean coast.

Under French law, any new building or flat can be joined to the mains system. The developer has the responsibility of making sure that a building conforms to the regulations and that the appropriate certificate (*certificat de conformité*) is issued for new property. This is handed over to EDF.

A deposit is required, which is refunded in portions after five and ten years. A second nominal charge is made for the meter when it is connected to the supply. In some circumstances a bond is required that can be set against future electricity bills.

Though supplies and installations may be cheap, some safety standards are not what we have come to expect in the UK. Watch out for:

- Insufficient power points, particularly in the kitchen. This is a chronic problem which seems peculiar to France. It even extends to the most recently-developed property where you will still find up to half a dozen low wattage appliances running from a multi-plug connector fed from a single socket.

- Unearthed electrical equipment. Dishwashers, driers, washing machines, and televisions are normally earthed. Special sockets are fitted to hobs, cookers and ovens.

- Timed earth trips. You sometimes have to wait several minutes after replacing a fuse before the normal supply is restored.

- Insecure light fittings and loose wall sockets with both bayonet and screw light fittings in the same room and sometimes even on the same wall.

- Some imported electrical equipment that is not compatible with the French 220 volt/50 cycle system, or not fitted with a slow start system. The power surge produced by turning on an imported electric kettle or microwave is often sufficient to blow the fuses or trip-switches.

- A multitude of plug and socket fittings, some unearthed, and almost all without fuses.

GAS

Gas in France is either town gas or bottled gas. Town gas is generally available in more densely populated urban areas and not at all in the countryside. It is supplied by state-owned Gaz de France (GDF). As elsewhere, gas prices have risen considerably in recent years.

If you buy a town property and wish to have it connected the charge is a little under €900 provided you are within 35 metres of the nearest supply point. There are four tariff options based on the number of cubic metres you are likely to use. This is calculated on the basis of factors such as whether or not gas is to be used for cooking, hot water and central heating. As in the UK (since 1992) the amount you actually use is converted into kilowatt hours for billing. Where gas is only used for cooking in shared buildings, the bills are paid by the *co-propriété* and added to individual service charges.

As electricity is cheap, visitors are often surprised to learn that most French homes have a back up (usually bottled) gas supply. Additionally there will often be a second (gas) hob fitted in the kitchen near to the electric one because electricity supplies are so regularly interrupted. Bottled gas is available at most garages and supermarkets. As in the UK, you are required to pay a container deposit. Propane is considered to be a better option than butane, although slightly less efficient, it is less affected by cold weather. In some rural areas it is possible to install garden-based gas tanks from companies such as Antargaz and Total. These are normally fitted free of charge in exchange for a supply contract of one year or more. One downside of this arrangement is an increase in insurance premiums.

WATER

French water is the most expensive in the world – typically around 60% more expensive than in the UK. Unlike the state monopolies of electricity and gas, all French is supplied by private companies. The largest of these – Cise, Lyonnaise des Eaux, Saur and Vivendi supply 80% of the market. If you have a septic tank, the bill will be reduced by up to 40%. Special rates apply for industrial and agricultural use, and for swimming pools.

Water supplies are metered. The meters are reliable and it is therefore difficult to question charges which vary from €2 to €5 per cubic metre (1,000 litres) depending on location. The psychological effect of metering explains why in France you will rarely see a domestic sprinkler system or hosepipe in operation.

Supply shortages are rare in urban areas, but common in rural areas during the summer. When water levels run low, the supply is simply turned off. Many rural homes have an emergency storage tank and keep grey (recycled house) water for the garden.

In central and southern France a significant number of properties are supplied by spring water or wells. The water is usually of excellent quality, and, best of all, virtually free.

LAND LINE TELEPHONES

Applications for a telephone are made to the local Agence Commerciale des Telecommunications or France Telecom. Installations have been known to take place the following day, but delays of up to 12 months are not unknown.

Those used to the UK's standard installation system are sometimes shocked by charges levied in France. Connections, particularly within a block of flats, are inexpensive, but if your home is several miles from existing connections, the charge will reflect the work involved.

The standard connection is called the *ligne mixte*. This is not a party line, but one that allows calls to be made in and out.

It is also worth noting:

- Ex-directory numbers are subject to a monthly surcharge.

- There are two phone books for each *département* – the *annuaire* (domestic listings) and the *professions* (yellow pages). The *annuaire* lists subscribers under towns and communes. The *professions* contains business listings and all those useful numbers that UK subscribers are used to finding in their standard phonebook.

- Lines may go silent between phases of dialling a number, and the ringing tone is frequently inaudible.

169

- Those used to the relative efficiency of BT may find its French equivalent – France Telecom (sometimes still referred to as 'PTT') – a source of frustration. Lines, particularly into the capital, are overloaded and regularly unavailable during office hours. Directory Enquiries has an abysmal record of giving correct numbers and checking overseas listings is often beyond them.

- As in the UK, a number of independent providers are now competing in the market place, but it can be similarly difficult to work out, on a like-for-like basis, what calls really cost. However, it is possible to make very cheap calls, particularly overseas, so the various tariff structures and suppliers (including www.telerabais.fr) are worth investigating.

- It is also worth investigating voice over internet protocol (VOIP) options – once broadband internet access is installed calls via the internet using, for example, www.skype.com or www.voipcheap.co.uk can be very cheap or even free.

INTERNET ACCESS

Broadband is being rolled out across the country although coverage in rural areas remains patchy. Technologically, France is ahead of Britain in terms of access speeds in many areas, with very high speeds available in most large cities. Many packages include free telephone calls and television access. Choosing an ISP is as difficult as elsewhere (www.grenouille.com is a useful website that lists all ISPs and their current performance levels), but once an order is placed for broadband access, the process can be refreshingly straightforward.

Mobile internet access in France is rather more developed with networks, such as Orange, already able to deliver access at download speeds comparable to standard land lines in the UK. There is a good range of internet cafés even in more remote areas which is useful when travelling, and many campsites also offer internet access via their own computers or using wifi as, of course, do most hotels.

MOBILE PHONES

Mobile phone coverage in France is excellent. This is partly because networks share cells, and partly because those living in the regions demand parity with Paris. You can generally log on to a network at the top of an Alp or at the bottom of a gorge. In military training areas, however, service can be suspended from time to time.

UK-bought mobiles theoretically work in France, but whether or not they do in practice depends on your sim card and contract. Advance line rental and monthly line rental contracts usually allow international roaming but 'Pay As You Talk' arrangements may not. Check with your service provider before you leave the UK. Do not assume that roaming has been automatically enabled. The same applies to mobile fax services.

Using your UK mobile in France is expensive – particularly between 07.00 and 19.00. Even off peak calls rapidly add up and text messages can cost as much as €1 each. Calls made to your mobile also appear on your bill. The provider you register with bills your UK network provider who adds a second round of charges and VAT before billing you. Some UK network providers – such as Vodafone – have been known to set their handsets to automatically locate the overseas providers with whom they have negotiated a mutually beneficial agreement. You can however search for alternative providers. Orange, a French company, is often considered the best mobile telephone service provider; messages, for instance, can be retrieved from anywhere in the world by pressing three digits and mobile internet links were both swifter and less likely to fail even before G3 technology was available.

A much more economic option is to swap your sim card with its French equivalent. Cards of the top-up variety, which naturally come with a French number, can be purchased (together with various introductory packages of free text and call time) from around €30. One slight problem is that if the phone is not used for a certain period (usually six months) your number (and card) becomes defunct and cannot be easily reinstated. And, once a French card is inserted, your phone loses its UK identity.

It is not at all uncommon for mobile owners to change cards each time they cross the channel.

SETTLING IN FRANCE

Although EC regulations have reduced the amount of documentation required for long stay visitors to member countries there are still a number of requirements in force.

PASSPORT

A standard EU passport is valid for ten years. No visa is required for tourists staying in France for up to three months. A person who stays for longer than three months is classified as resident.

CARTE DE SÉJOUR

The *visa de longue durée* (long stay visa) no longer exists although it is still referred to, even by officials. It has been superseded by the '*Carte de Séjour de ressortissant de l'Union Européeanne*' (EU resident permit). If you intend to become resident in France you have three months from entering the country to apply for your EU '*Carte de Séjour*'.

You will require:

- A valid passport and three further passport photographs.

- Proof that you have residential accommodation.

- Proof that you pay into the French Social Security scheme.

- Proof of means of support. In practice this means either a contract of employment, or evidence of self-employment (from the local Chamber of Commerce), or evidence of a state pension or other recognised pension.

- Birth and marriage certificates.

If you are staying for a 'limited duration', a resident permit will be issued for this period of time, after which you will be re-assessed. If you are planning to stay on a 'permanent' basis, a resident permit will be issued for five years. After five years your permit can normally be renewed for a further ten years (and so on). According to the guidelines (www.ambafrance-uk.org) this 'right of residence' granted by the permit can be extended to the permit holder's spouse, dependant descendants (under 21), dependant ascendant and the spouse's ascendants.

FRENCH CITIZENSHIP

Long-term residents sometimes choose to take French citizenship because foreigners may be subject to a heavier burden of personal taxation. It is also possible, even prudent, to take the view that if you are to benefit from the French health and welfare systems it is better to be working towards French citizenship. The rules are that you must:

- Have lived in France for at least five years. For the spouses of people who already hold French citizenship and their children, this regulation does not apply.

- Be more than 18 years of age.

- Have no criminal record.

- Prove that you can speak and write in French to a reasonable standard.

MANAGING THE REMOVAL

Moving within the UK can be a stressful experience, but taking your property to France can be doubly so. A DIY removal is not recommended. Larger UK companies have a great deal of experience of the process, although employing this expertise can be pricey, it is nevertheless recommended. But shop around. Recent quotes for a removal from Coventry to Carcassone varied by as much as €2,500. Equally quotes for storage for a typical three-packing-case property varied from €250 a month to almost three times as much. It may be possible to do a special storage deal with the company who will ultimately manage your removal.

Import Regulations

Household goods and personal effects can normally be imported into France duty free, nevertheless there are a number of regulations, the breach of any of which can create considerable delay.

Firearms may not be imported unless a special application has been processed. Details are available from consulates.

A full inventory of goods (three copies) should be presented to customs officers when the goods are first taken to France. Property can then be imported in 'lots', but there is a time limitation (before import tax is imposed) of 12 months. It is important that you have certification (or can identify labels) to prove that foam furniture is fire retardant.

Goods should correspond to the financial status of the owner; customs will be suspicious of someone with a modest income importing a valuable collection of antiques. It is prudent to provide some form of proof of purchase for items of exceptional value.

175

You will also require a change of residence certificate from the *mairie* of the district you are moving to. Additionally a declaration of *non-cession* (non-transfer) is required. This is a statement that your household goods come within the duty-free regulations. You may also have to demonstrate that furnishings meet fire retardant standards, it is worth observing that some items are stamped on the underside.

If your French property is to be used as a holiday home or secondary residence, additional rules apply.

It is these last rules that most frequently cause difficulty. Basically, they state that all goods must have been owned and used by the importer for three months before the removal date and that they should be appropriate for usage in a secondary residence. The French would naturally prefer you to buy your goods in their country and they have been known to discourage imports. As most furniture and electrical goods are cheaper in the UK there is a natural temptation to take in as much as you can.

The best way to avoid problems is to make purchases four to six months before import and to keep receipts. Electrical goods, especially if presented to customs in original packing, are most likely to provoke comment.

PETS

Since the pilot scheme was introduced in 2000, it has been possible to transport pets within the EC (and more recently the US and Canada) providing they fulfil the regulations. Briefly these are:

- Each animal must be micro-chipped to meet agreed EU standards.

- The animal must have had an anti-rabies injection and blood tests must show the antibodies in the animal's blood.

- Six months must have elapsed from the successful blood test to the date of departure.

Initial costs will be about €350 per animal and then bi-annually a further anti-rabies injection must be given.

Animals which have successfully fulfilled the above obligations can then be taken to France through approved ports of embarkation and disembarkation.

Those wishing to return to the UK with their pets must visit a French vet between 24 and 48 hours before departure to have the animal treated for ticks, fleas and worms and the relevant documents completed. This typically costs around €30.

Rules on animal imports are likely to change at short notice. In the UK the Department for Food and Rural Affairs have a special PETS help line (0870 241 1710), or visit the DEFRA website at: http://www.defra.gov.uk.

At present you are allowed to import up to three domestic animals into France, but only one of them may be a puppy or an animal under six months old. The date at which a French vaccination certificate is required is twelve months from the issue of the UK equivalent, and not, as popularly thought, twelve months after the animal is imported to France.

French law requires dogs to have annual anti-rabies vaccinations. The number of the certificate must be tattooed into the dog's ear. British regulations have been amended to cover dogs that have been tattooed, then micro-chipped and have the relevant vaccine certificates. These animals can then be re-imported to Britain.

HEALTH CARE

EHIC

All citizens of EU member states are entitled to health care in other member states as well as in the European Economic Area, which includes Iceland, Liechtenstein, Norway and Switzerland.

Until recently you required an Eform – such as an E111 or E128. Those who applied for these forms after July 2004, and who have subsequently remained resident at the address from which they applied, should already have been added to the national database and their new card – the EHIC – should by now have been issued.

The new EHIC is available through national social security systems. The card entitles you to 'necessary' health care in the public system if you become ill or injured, but may not provide the full cost of health care. Further, the card does not cover the cost of repatriation or ongoing or continuing care for chronic conditions other than those specified such as serious such as diabetes. The EHIC may also not cover someone who 'decides' to have treatment for a chronic condition in another member state. This, however, is currently a matter of legal interpretation. There have been cases, for instance, when a person who has been waiting for treatment 'beyond a reasonable time' has successfully recovered part of the cost of 'necessary treatment' in another EC country.

In theory, the question of reimbursement for medical costs will remain as before the introduction of the EHIC. In practice much of the former chaos remains. You may still have to pay for your treatment at the point of delivery and then claim a refund in the UK. And that refund may not necessarily cover the full cost of the treatment.

The card has courted controversy, not least because it is seen as another step towards federalism. Ultimately a common model of the card – featuring the EC logo – is to be applied. It will be a smartcard, which could contain medical records and, perhaps, iris recognition data. There are not, however, presently in existence technological systems that allow the interchange of this kind of information beyond national boundaries.

Paying for medical top-up insurance is highly recommended.

Medicines

Short-stay visitors (those who have not applied for a *carte de séjour*) should take an adequate supply of regularly-required medication with them. Each medicine should be labelled with both its generic and trade name, and dosages should be clearly indicated.

NHS doctors are encouraged to supply only limited quantities of medicines, so if you intend to be out of the UK for more than a month you will need certificate E112 to get further supplies in France. Enclose a covering letter from your doctor and write to:

Department of Health
Overseas Branch
Richmond House
79 Whitehall
London SW1A 2NL
(0207 210 4850)

Some pharmaceutical products are marketed in France with different brand names and others are formulated slightly differently. In some cases (particularly for patients suffering from a heart condition) it is best to arrange for an imported supply of medication. Doctors can give long-term prescriptions to UK pharmacists who can arrange for dispatch in sealed packaging together with the appropriate customs declaration. You should expect to pay around extra €3 per package in addition to normal prescription charges.

It is worth remembering that French pharmacists, like their English counterparts, offer good advice on simple medicines like pain killers, mosquito repellents or those offering relief from cold symptoms.

Mail delivery times between France and the UK are notoriously irregular. It may be wise to retain several days' emergency supply of regularly-used medication.

Dental and Eye Care

French dentists and opticians are amongst the best qualified in Europe.

Replacing spectacles and contact lenses is straightforward if you have a copy of your prescription. Failing that, a phone call or email to the UK can quickly remedy the situation. A new eye test will be automatically carried out if the prescription is more than five years old (three years for those over 70 years of age).

There is a special 'dial a dentist' service for emergency home treatment, and for those staying in temporary accommodation. Charges are made and reclaimed in the same way as for other medical services.

Health Care for Residents

If you become resident in France you can choose to make voluntary contributions to the *Securité Sociale* which administers the French Health Service. If you are retired (and in receipt of the UK state pension) you are, theoretically, entitled to health care without making a contribution. Form E121 is required to prove this entitlement. Residents, whether retired or not, should seek a more permanent solution. Again, this will inevitably include top-up health insurance.

Choosing a Doctor

As in the UK you are theoretically entitled to choose your own medical practitioner. In practice this may also mean registering at a local health centre or clinic.

However, French doctors are more likely than their UK counterparts to be working independently. Some are similar to our GPs, but the majority offer an additional, specialist qualification. This specialist work is the most lucrative, so French practitioners make a concerted effort to promote this area of their work. Choosing a doctor is therefore not as straightforward as in the UK. Yellow pages may help, but personal recommendation is better.

Take family documentation to the *Relations Internationales* department of the *Securité Sociale*. This should include passports and marriage certificates, including translations.

The *Relations Internationales* department are unable to recommend any individual doctor or practice. They do, however, provide information about many aspects of health care, and they hold lists of practitioners, together with their specialisms.

Medical Insurance

The French private health scheme is called the Mutuelle. By joining you can reclaim any payment you have made for medical charges. In most cases you are claiming back from the Health Service the difference of approximately 25% of total treatment charges that you have had to find from your own pocket. In certain circumstances (such as disability) it is possible to claim a supplementary or top-up pension. Again the *Relations Internationales* department will be able to explain the rules to you.

The French *Securité Sociale* is a network of organisations that provide welfare benefits which are more extensive than their UK equivalents. Joining the scheme is expensive, so private medical insurance is well worth considering and this is often cheapest and simplest to arrange in the UK. However, insurers may question a claim made from France unless you make your intentions clear on the proposal form. It is also worth checking the wording of the policy for limitations and exclusions sometimes applied to extended illnesses and chronic medical problems.

MOTORING

The Driver and the Law

The essentials are:

- You have to be over 18 with a full licence, to drive in France.

- The French drive on the right.

- It is a legal requirement to carry a red warning triangle, high-visibility jackets, spare bulbs, a first aid kit and a fire extinguisher.

- Third party insurance is compulsory.

- Driving documents, including your licence and vehicle registration document, must be available for inspection.

You are advised to carry a *constat* – a specially printed form to be filled in immediately after an accident. This can prevent difficulties with insurance claims, especially if there is hidden damage to your vehicle.

French roads are designated as motorways (A for *autoroute*), *routes nationales* (N roads, rather like our 'A' roads) and *routes departmentales* (D roads). Most motorways are toll roads with a speed limit of 130 kph, but this reduces to 110 kph in wet weather. 110 kph is the norm for dual carriageways, 90 kph for single carriageways, and 50 kph in urban areas. *Routes Nationales* are less busy than their British equivalents.

Speed limits are rigorously enforced by traffic police. Toll cards are time stamped and there are both radar and camera speed traps, although these are much less frequent than in the UK. For minor offences (*contraventions*) police can impose a fixed penalty fine (*amende forfaitaire*).

This fixed penalty scheme includes:

- Not using seat belts, carrying a child under ten in the front seat, illegal use of the horn, and causing an obstruction – all about €20.

- Dangerous parking or parking at a bus stop, careless driving, ignoring signs and priority rules, speeding, and failing to stop at a traffic light – all about €140.

- Failure to pay fixed penalty fines within 30 days means the offence is reclassified as *une amende majorée*. These are dealt with through the courts and fine levels are increased by 120%.

The legal limit for drinking and driving is lower than in the UK and the law is applied in much the same way. The French penalty system however is ruthless. Despite this severity, French driving behaviour, especially in busy towns, can create the impression that there is no law at all and accident statistics during peak holiday periods make horrific reading. Recently more rigorous enforcement of both drinking and speeding laws have dramatically improved accident statistics.

Driving Licence

The British driving licence used to be valid in France for 12 months, after which you were required to apply for a French one. However, an EU Driving Licence Directive now requires the mutual recognition of all driving licences issued within the EU.

In theory this means you will not require a French licence. However, since 1992, the French have operated a complex and controversial system in respect of motoring offences.

Holders of French licences begin with 12 points which are deducted according to the severity of offences. Deductions range from one point for failing to dip headlights to six for driving under the influence of alcohol. When all 12 points are lost you forfeit your licence. Points are normally restored three years after conviction. It is also much more common in France to have your licence temporarily suspended for between seven and 28 days.

Those who are subject to a resident's permit and who also commit a motoring offence in France are required to obtain a French driving licence so that the points system can be applied to them. As the application process takes at least two months and the UK licence has to be surrendered with the application for the French one, you could just find yourself in a legal minefield. Worse still, the French and British authorities are now cooperating to make offences committed in one country accountable in the other. However, at the present time, the French police do not serve fixed penalty notices incurred in the UK on the owners of vehicles bearing French plates. If however your vehicle has UK plates and you fall foul of a UK speed camera you will not escape the penalty simply by returning to France.

If you are likely to be spending more time in France than the UK it is therefore recommended that you apply for a French licence as soon as you receive your resident's permit. To make the application you will require your UK licence with a translation, your resident's permit, proof of domicile and two passport photographs. The French issuing authority is the *Service du Permis de Conduire de la Prefecture de Police*.

Importing a Vehicle

If you import your vehicle you will need French licence plates (*plaques d'immatriculation*) after six months. You apply to the *Prefecture de Police* who send you a number and a local garage will make up and fit the plate for a modest fee.

Vehicle owners are also required to obtain registration documents for the vehicle (the *carte grise*). A *carnet de passage en douanes* (certificate of passage through customs) is a further document to retain if you are considering importing the vehicle.

The Carte Grise

The *carte grise* is the equivalent of a UK registration document.

Contrôle Technique

The French roadworthiness test is similar to the UK MOT. Passing the roadworthiness test is required to renew car insurance.

Duty

French residents (and temporary residents) who import their vehicles from the UK within 12 months can do so tax free.

There is no set limit on the number of vehicles that can be imported. The rule is they must have been the personal property of the resident for six months prior to import and they cannot be sold for six months after the import date.

If you intend to import a vehicle you will require documentation from a French consulate in the UK.

Buying a Vehicle in France

There are advantages to this:

- New vehicle prices remain a touch lower in France despite the UK's recent price reductions.

- For up to six months you can run the vehicle on temporary (TT) plates if you pay in foreign currency.

- Left hand drive vehicles are safer to drive and easier to sell in France, although they can be very difficult to sell in the UK. There are some small, but significant parts for RHD vehicles that are difficult, or impossible to obtain in France. Accelerator cables, for instance, are invariably a different length.

- Second hand values tend to be higher in France than in the UK.

Vehicle Insurance

In the short term you can extend your UK cover by asking your insurers for an international insurance certificate (green card). For this you may pay a modest supplementary premium or administration fee. Motor insurance for unlimited third-party liability is compulsory in France and premiums are relatively expensive because of a large number of accidents and the number of stolen vehicles.

The French vehicle insurance market is also fairly complex. There are five basic types of policy in force – from third party only (legal minimum cover) to fully comprehensive with driver protection –

which adds special cover for incapacity arising from injury.

Premiums are loaded against drivers under the age of 25 and those who have been convicted of drunken or dangerous driving. All vehicles worth more than €15,000 must have the registration number engraved on the windows and have an alarm fitted. Vehicles not securely garaged overnight are surcharged. No claims bonuses of up to a maximum 50% can be earned after ten years. UK earned bonuses can be transferred for up to this amount provided there is written evidence (not a renewal notice) from a UK insurer. If you hold the maximum bonus for three years, one accident will not reduce it. Many French insurers also require a translation. No-claims bonuses are lost if you do not hold vehicle insurance for a period of two years.

Claims, which must be submitted within five days of an incident, are generally dealt with on the basis of reports from the police and the drivers concerned. If you are judged to be less than 30% responsible your bonus will not be affected. Repairs are normally sanctioned by insurance assessors. When a vehicle is reported stolen the claim will not be considered for 30 days.

BANKING IN FRANCE

A British Account

Even if you intend to live in France it is well worth considering retaining a British bank account – or at least until the UK embraces (if ever) the euro. If nothing else, this will save the cost of currency exchange when visiting Britain.

Although it is theoretically possible for residents to manage without a French bank account, it is undoubtedly more convenient to have one. French banking rules are, however, rather different from those in most other EC countries. It is best to be aware of the way the system works.

UK Banks in France

All the major UK banks are represented in France, although outside the major cities the branches are thinly distributed.

The advantage of dealing with a UK bank in France is primarily one of communication. Banks of all nationalities are subject to French banking law.

Opening a Bank Account

Foreigners can open a special account called a *compte étranger* (literally a stranger's account). Sterling can be paid in by normal bank transfer methods, or by cheque or cash. The French government has sought to reduce tax evasion by discouraging 'cash' deals which means that French notes and coinage cannot be paid into bank accounts.

The *compte étranger* can be an ordinary/current account (*compte cheques*) or a deposit account (*compte sur livret*). The ordinary account provides you with a cheque book, and the deposit account pays interest. Orders for new cheque books can take several weeks to process, so it is best to keep a spare book.

Arrangements for statements are similar to those in force in the UK, but it is unwise to assume that your statement is up to date. There are good reasons why the French clearing system is referred to as *la tortue* – the tortoise. Most banks provide access to accounts via the internet and this is probably the best way to monitor balances.

When you open an account, the bank will check with central records to find out if you are subject to an *interdiction* – a ban from holding a bank account. Inter-bank communication is excellent; a UK bankruptcy, a withdrawal of credit notice, or a court order for debt or non payment, will almost certainly prevent you from opening an ordinary account.

Interest

Gross interest is paid on deposit accounts. It is your responsibility to declare this to the tax authorities either in France or the UK. The double taxation agreement between the countries means that you are only liable to pay tax once.

Most banks impose a minimum balance for ordinary accounts – usually around €100. Interest is not ordinarily paid on these accounts unless you agree to maintain a higher minimum balance.

Credits and Debits

Cheques paid into your account are credited on the same day, even if post-dated, but you cannot draw against them until clearance is complete.

French cheques are similar to those in the UK with the amount written in both words and numbers; if the amounts are different, the words will be assumed to be correct. Cheques must be endorsed; open cheques will be honoured but this can lead to delay; crossed cheques are recommended. Cheques can only be stopped for security reasons – this generally means notifying the bank that it has been lost or stolen.

Using and Misusing Cheques

French law allows traders to refuse a cheque for any amount less than €15, and cash for any amount greater than that, but both events are rare. Indeed, as part of the continued battle against 'cash' deals, French law now insists that cheques are issued as payment for work or services valued at more than €150. The law has recently been extended to apply to rents and office supplies.

Cheque guarantee cards are not issued in France, but some form of proof of identity is likely to be required. French nationals carry identity cards.

The French are tough on misuse of bank accounts. If you bounce a cheque the bank will instruct you to put matters right and, if you fail to do so within the 30 day time limit, your cheque book will be withdrawn, the account frozen and you will be subject to a ban (an *interdiction*). The ban is recorded with the Banque de France and the file is retained for two years, during which time you may not open or operate a bank account in France. Even if your account is regularised within 30 days, a second offence within the year will incur a 12 month cheque book ban.

Financial penalties for bouncing cheques are severe. These can range from a fine of €450 to €40,000. Prison sentences of up to five years can be (and occasionally are) imposed. Misunderstanding the system, or claiming the problem arose through the slowness of the clearing system have not proved to be adequate defences in law.

Bank Dispensers and Credit Cards

Bank dispensers (*distributeurs*) are similar to those operating in the UK, with the additional advantage that many offer English language for transactions. Some dispensers do not accept metallic-strip cards which have now largely been replaced by 'chip and pin'. The problem is exacerbated by the fact that French 'chip and pin' technology is out of step with much of the rest of Europe – including the UK. This is because the French introduced their own technology long before it was generally applied elsewhere. The French are committed to coming into line, but it is uncertain how long this may take. To make matters worse, UK debit cards (such as 'Switch') are virtually useless in France other than for use in *distributeurs*. The remedy, for the time being, is to carry a number of credit cards which have both the metallic strip and pin embedded. Supermarkets, in particular, do not like to lose a sale and you will eventually find a card that works. Increasingly, UK chip and pin cards are being found to work in French shops and banks.

Credit card companies monitor transactions in order to limit fraud. If a card, which has not been used outside the UK for some time, is suddenly used for cash withdrawals in France it may be 'flagged'. If your card is rejected by a number of French bank dispensers this is possibly the reason. Check with your credit card issuer, or, better still, inform them of time periods when you intend to use the card, for cash withdrawals, outside the UK.

For a modest fee French banks will issue a *carte de retrait* (withdrawal card). Much better (but pricier) is a *carte de paiement national* which allows withdrawals from any dispenser in the Carte Bancaire group which includes most of the major banks. Carte Bancaire dispensers are identified by the distinctive CB logo.

Cash dispensers can be found on high streets and at strategic points close to hypermarkets and shopping precincts.

TAXATION

The basic taxes for individuals are:

- Income tax. This is divided in French law into earned income (*impot sur le revenue*) and unearned income (*impot des revenues des capitaux mobliers*).

- Land tax (*taxe foncière*).

- Community tax (*taxe d'habitation*).

- Capital gains tax (*régime des plus values des particuliers*).

- Death duties (*droits de succession*).

- Gift tax (*droits de donation*).

Registration

The ownership of all properties must be registered with the French tax authorities. Owners who are not resident have to register by 30th April following completion of the property purchase. Residents are expected to register immediately with the local *Centre des Impots*. Non-resident owners should register with the Tax Centre for Non Residents at:

Centre des Impots des Non-residents
9 Rue D'Uzes
75094 Paris

Domicile

For international tax purposes the concept of domicile is important. Those who have their fiscal domicile in one country theoretically pay tax in that country on their income. There is, however, some give and take on this. Some pensions, for instance, originating in the UK, are automatically taxed there.

Those considered to be domiciled outside France pay tax only on that portion of their income earned in France. You will be said to have a French fiscal domicile if:

- You have a home in France and spend more than 183 days in France in any financial year.

- Your spouse and family live in France for more than 183 days in any financial year, even if you spend most of your time out of the country.

- You work in France on either a salaried or self-employed basis, unless you can prove that work is ancillary to your main employment.

- Most of your income is generated in France. This could for instance catch retired people who run a successful *gîte* business.

Income Tax

If you are domiciled in France you are liable to pay income tax. Even if you are not domiciled, you remain liable for tax on income earned in France; this would, for instance, include income from a *gîte* business. The French tax laws are complex and there will be winners and losers in comparison with the UK system.

Long-term residents frequently choose to take French citizenship because foreigners are subject to an increasingly heavy burden of personal taxation. Set against this, however, is the fact that in many situations a tax burden can be reduced by paying as much tax as possible (tax on public service pensions, for instance) in the UK. Equally, you can legitimately set personal allowances against your income in both countries. Indeed there is a whole range of scenarios where a favourable outcome is achieved by being 100% honest.

French income tax is assessed on a family basis. The husband is responsible for the return which includes the income of his wife and children who are still in the educational system, or doing their military service. Divorced, separated or widowed persons claim allowances according to circumstances. Across the board allowances include:

- Money spent on major property repairs.

- Money spent on certain 'green projects' such as the installation of solar energy panels for heating.

- Payments for maintenance and dependent relatives other than children.

- Gifts to certain charities.

- Contributions to the *Securité Sociale*.

- Approved life assurance premiums.

- Interest payments on certain loans.

- Special arrangements for single parents with young children.

The French income tax system benefits large families and those on relatively low incomes. The tax year runs from January 1st each year and bills are paid in three equal instalments in the year following the liability.

Filling in a tax return is difficult because of the complexity of the system and the amount of technical language involved. English-speaking residents paying income tax in France invariably require the services of an accountant.

When the authorities suspect that tax declarations are inaccurate or fraudulent they will investigate. In certain circumstances residents with complex tax affairs (including perhaps income from a number of sources outside France) will be assessed according to the punitive *régime de d'imposition forfaiture*. Using this system income is assessed according to arbitrary norms which includes ascribing a letting value to all properties you own and multiplying it by a factor of three or five. Cars are valued and taxed at 75% of maximum new showroom value, servants are assumed to have massive salaries, and race horses are reckoned to be winners.

The system is rarely applied, but it demonstrates what can happen to those who fall foul of the tax authorities.

Land Tax

Taxe foncière is levied by the local commune and is very similar to the system of parish rates in the UK. Registers of all property and owners are maintained at the *mairie*.

Property is given a notional letting value on which the *taxe foncière* is based. Exceptions include government and public buildings, grain stores, wine presses and stables. New buildings are exempt from the tax for two years.

The last general valuation of buildings was carried out in 1974. The tax levied is adjusted annually in line with the index of inflation.

Community Tax

Taxe d'habitation is paid by the resident occupier of a property on January 1st each year. It is calculated according to the value of amenities. These include the size of the property, including garages, outbuildings and land. If the property is not subject to a lease, then the owner of the property is liable for the payment of the tax.

The base rate of the tax is calculated again on the notional letting value of the property, last calculated in 1987 and up-rated since then by indexation.

This tax is reduced when the property is used as the principal residence of a family. Since 1989 each commune has fixed *taxe d'habitation* at rates of five, ten or 15% of the rentable value.

Both *taxe foncière* and *taxe d'habitation* are payable by UK residents whether or not the property is designated as their main residence. But even taken together they rarely amount to 65% of the average UK Council Tax Band D. In France it is national rather than local taxation that really hurts.

Capital Gains Tax

The *régime de plus value des particuliers* is imposed on anyone who is domiciled in France when assets are sold, but their primary residence is exempted. The tax is invariably applied to those selling French property who are domiciled abroad.

The tax is levied at 16%. The capital gain is deemed to be the difference between purchase price and sale price, but the seller can offset:

- The supplementary costs of making the purchase, or ten per cent of the purchase price – whichever is the higher figure.

- An indexation of the increase in property values calculated according to government figures.

French law demands that foreign sellers employ an agent to handle the sale. This agent (normally a *notaire*) is responsible for paying the tax to the government. It is possible to get clearance for payment before completion; this is highly recommended as it saves time and paperwork and will reduce the fee the agent charges for his services.

In practice the capital gains tax payable on a property sale is likely to be modest or non-existent for many sellers. Those who improve property considerably, or create new residential units (such as an integral independent granny flat) are most likely to find themselves paying for the privilege. The tax is designed to catch foreigners who are systematically renovating French property for profit.

Inheritance Tax

French law is very concerned with the idea of passing down assets within a family. The concept is called *patrimoine* and it is the guiding principle of *droits de succession*. The main elements of *patrimoine* are that:

- Payments are made by those who inherit, according to the value of assets they receive and their relationship to the deceased. The closest relationships suffer the smallest tax burden. A son would therefore receive more of the inheritance than a nephew and so on. Special rules apply to surviving spouses.

- All assets in France are subject to *droits de succession*. The assets of those domiciled in France include property at home and abroad.

- The assets of those not domiciled in France exclude property outside the country. Double tax agreements with other countries ensure that *droits de succession* paid in France are exempted from tax liability elsewhere.

The French rules of inheritance, particularly with regard to the entitlement of surviving spouses, have been simplified recently, but owners of property in France are well advised to have a will drawn up by a *notaire*. This may now include a special contract called a *communaute universelle*. Another possibility is to invest in a special kind of *assurance vie* in which you name beneficiaries, which has the effect of ensuring that up to €147,000 is free of French inheritance tax.

Gift Tax

The rules for *droits de donation* are similar to those applied above. The idea is to prevent the avoidance of inheritance tax.

There is some mitigation for:

• Gifts given as wedding presents.

• Gifts made by people under the age of 65.

Value Added Tax

There are presently three rates of *Taxe sur la Valeur Ajoutée* (*TVA*) in France:

• 5.5% for most agricultural and food products, transport, entertainment and some principal-residence improvements.

• A standard rate of 19.6% for most other items.

• 2.1% for medicaments, some entertainments and some publications.

The sale of new properties (or any first sale within five years of construction) is subject to TVA. This will always be included in the sale price and will be paid by the developer.

Any property re-sold within that five year period is also subject to TVA. This concerns UK buyers more than is necessary as the amount is not usually considerable because the seller offsets the amount paid in TVA on the initial sale, and French property values generally advance more cautiously than those in Britain. Only when a property has been substantially improved or modified during the five year period is it likely to attract a significant TVA bill.

The French Property Restorer's Essential French Phrasebook

French	English	English	French
acquéreur	purchaser	accountant	*comptable*
aggloméré	chipboard	adhesive (for tiles)	*cément colle*
agrafe	window catch	advice	*conseils*
agrandissement	extension	alter or convert	*aménager*
alimentation	supply or supplier	amount (of money)	*montant*
alimentation en eau	water supply	approximately	*environ*
aménager	to alter or convert	asbestos	*amiante*
amiante	asbestos	attic	*grenier*
appui	sill	authority (documented)	*pouvoir*
armature	a reinforcement	balcony	*balcon*
assainissement	disposal of sewage	ballcock	*robinet à flotteur*
bac à gâcher	mixing tray (e.g. plaster)	banisters	*rampe d'escalier*
bac de douche	shower tray	bankruptcy	*faillite*
bâche	tarpaulin	bathroom	*salle de bains*
bâcier	to botch	batten or bracket	*liteau*
balcon	balcony	bedroom	*chambre*
ballon d'eau	water tank	bill (utility)	*facture*
bâtiment	building	blade	*lame*
bêche	spade	bolt	*boulon*
bénéfice	profit	botch	*bâcier*
benne	rubbish skip	boundary (limit)	*borne*

béton armé	reinforced concrete	breeze block	*parpaing aggloméré*
béton prêt a l'emploi	ready-mixed concrete	brick (standard)	*brique pleine*
bétonnière	concrete mixer	brush (wire)	*brosse métallique*
blocaille	rubble	building	*bâtiment*
bois contraplaqué	plywood	bungalow	*plain pied*
bon bricolage	may good fortune shine on your DIY efforts	business (name and goodwill)	*fonds de commerce*
borne	boundary (limit)	business (venture)	*entreprise*
boulon	bolt	cable	*câble*
brique plain	standard brick	carpet	*moquette*
brosse métallique	wire brush	carry out (agreement)	*realisation*
brouette	wheelbarrow	ceiling	*plafond*
cabinet	small room or office	ceiling (false)	*faux plafond*
capitaux permanents	long term finances (resources)	cellar	*sous sol*
cellier	store (room)	chimney (and fireplace)	*cheminée*
cément colle	adhesive for tiles	chimney stack	*souche*
chambre	bedroom	chipboard	*aggloméré*
chape	screed	chippings	*gravillons*
charges	expenses, costs	clerk of works	*maître d'ouvrage*
charnière	hinge	concrete mixer	*bétonnière*
chauffage	heating	concrete, ready-mixed	*béton prêt à l'emploi*

chauffage central	central heating	concrete, reinforced	*béton armé*
cheminée	chimney or fireplace	conservatory	*jardin d'hiver*
cheville	wall plug	construction	*construction*
chevron	rafter	cornice	*corniche*
chute descente	downpipe	covered	*couvert*
citerne	tank	damp (proof) course	*couche méable*
clé	spanner	deadline	*délai d'execution*
cloison	partition	deadline	*délai*
clou	nail	delivery date	*délai de livraison*
commerçant	trader (legal and licensed)	deposit	*dépôt de garantie*
commune	district (local)	district (local)	*commune*
comptable	accountant	DIY	*bricolage*
conduit	cable	double glazing	*double vitrage*
construction	construction	downpipe	*chute descente*
contenance	land area	drain (main)	*grand collecteur*
corniche	cornice	drainage (mains)	*tout-à-l'égout*
couche méable	damp (proof) course	draw up a contract	*rediger un contrat*
coulis	grout	drill (pneumatic)	*marteau piquer*
couvert	covered	dry rot	*pourriture*
cuisine	kitchen	earth (electrical)	*terre sol*
dalle	flagstone	estimate	*devis*
débarras	box room	excavator	*pelleteuse*

201

délai	deadline	extension	*agrandisssement*
délai d'execution	deadline	fault	*malfaçon*
délai de livraison	delivery date	fibreglass	*fibre de verre*
délai de reflexion	pause for thought	finances, long term resources	*capitaux permanents*
dépôt de garantie	deposit	finishing	*finition*
devis	estimate	fireplace (and chimney)	*cheminée*
double vitrage	double glazing	fittings (taps and bath)	*robinetterie*
durée	time period (mortgage)	flagstone	*dalle*
échafaudage	scaffolding	floor (covering)	*revêtement de sol*
élément de cuisine	kitchen unit	floor joist	*solive de plancher*
entreprise	business (venture)	floorboard	*planche*
environ	approximately	floorboard (warped)	*planche voilée*
escalier	staircase	flue (metal liner)	*tubage*
étage	storey	foundations (+ main walls)	*gros oeuvre*
etancheite	imperviousness	frame (iron, for concreting)	*férraillage*
extérieur	outside	french window	*porte-fenêtre*
facture	invoice, bill(utility)	garden	*jardin*
faillite	bankruptcy	glazing	*vitrage*
faux plafond	false ceiling	ground	*sol*
fenêtre	window	grounds	*terrain*
fenêtre à guillotine	sash window	grout	*coulis*

férraillage	iron frame (for concreting)	gun (glue)	*pistolet à colle*
fibre de verre	fibreglass	gun (sealant or silicone)	*pistolet pour mastic*
finition	finishing	hammer	*marteau*
flexion	sagging	heating	*chauffage*
fonds de commerce	business (name and goodwill)	heating (central)	*chauffage central*
fosse septique	septic tank	hinge	*charnière*
four	oven	home (second)	*maison secondaire*
gazonner	to put down turf	house	*maison*
géomètre	survey or surveyor	house (detached)	*pavillon*
grand collecteur	main drain	imperviousness	*étanchéité*
gravillons	chippings	infilling (cracks)	*rebouchage*
grenier	attic	insulation (heat)	*isolation thermique*
grès	sandstone	insulation (panel)	*panneau composite*
gros oeuvre	walls and foundations	insulation (sound)	*isolation acoustique*
hors d'équerre	not (or out of) square	interior	*intérieur*
hourder	to render	invoice	*facture*
hypothèque	mortgage	ironmonger's	*quincaillerie*
indivision	joint (property) ownership	joinery	*ménuiserie*
isolation acoustique	sound insulation	joist (steel)	*solive en acier*

isolation thermique	heat insulation	kitchen	*cuisine*
jardin	garden	kitchen unit	*élément de cuisine*
jardin d'hiver	conservatory	land, building	*terrain constructible*
jointoiement	pointing	lawn	*pelouse*
jouissance	right to tenure	lay (bricks)	*maçonner*
laine d'acier	wire wool	lender	*organisme prêteur*
laine de roche	rockwool	loans and mortgages	*prêts*
lame	blade	lounge (living room)	*living/salle de séjour/salon*
liteau	batten or bracket	manhole cover	*plaque d'égout*
living	lounge (living room)	masonry mortar	*mortier normal*
maçonner	to lay bricks	mildew	*moisissure*
maison	house	mortar	*mortier*
maison d'amis	second home	mortgage	*hypothèque*
maître d'ouvrage	clerk of works	mortgage (period)	*durée*
malfaçon	fault	moulding	*moulure*
marteau	hammer	nail	*clou*
marteau piquer	pneumatic drill	offer (to buy)	*offre d'achat*
mastiquer	to putty	out of true (alignment)	*porter a faux*
menuiserie	joinery	outside	*extérieur*
mètre ruban	tape for measuring	oven	*four*
moisissure	mildew	overflow (pipe or drain)	*tuyeu de trop-plein*
montant	amount (of money)	ownership, joint (property)	*indivision*

moquette	carpet	paint (work)	*peinture*
mortier	mortar	partition	*cloison*
mortier normal	masonry	pause *(for thought)*	délai de reflexion
moulure	moulding	permit for building	*permis de construire*
mur de retenue	retaining wall	plasterboard	*placoplâtre*
offre d'achat	offer to buy	plywood	*bois contraplaqué*
organisme prêteur	lender	pointing	*jointoiement*
ouverture de chantier	start of (building) work	postponement	*remise*
panneau composite	insulation panel	power point	*prise de courant*
parpaing	breeze block	price (fixed)	*prix fixe*
pavillon	small(ish) detached house	profit	*bénéfice*
peinture	paint (work)	purchaser	*acquéreur*
peleteuse	excavator	to putty	*mastiquer*
pelouse	lawn	rafter	*chevron*
permis de construire	permit for building	reconditioning	*remise en état*
pièce	room	reinforcement, a	*armature*
pistolet à colle	glue gun	render	*hourder*
pistolet pour mastic	sealant (silicone) gun	resurface	*refaire la surface*
placage	veneer	rockwool	*laine de roche*
placoplâtre	plasterboard	roof	*toiture*

plafond	ceiling	room	*pièce*
plain-pied	single storey	room (small)	*cabinet*
planche	board (floor)	room (store)	*cellier*
planche voilée	warped floorboard	room (box)	*débarras*
plaque d'égout	manhole cover	room (living)	*salle de séjour*
plinthe	skirting	room (sitting)	*salon*
poncer	to rub down	rub down	*poncer*
ponceuse	sanding machine	rubble	*blocaille*
porte-fenêtre	french window	sagging	*flexion*
porter à faux	out of true (alignment)	sander (machine)	*ponceuse*
poser une vitre	put in a window	sandstone	*grès*
pourriture	dry rot	saw	*scie*
pouvoir	authority (documented)	scaffolding	*échafaudage*
préscriptions	instruction advice	screed	*chape*
prêts	loans and mortgages	screw	*vis*
prise de courant	power point	screwdriver	*tournevis*
prix fermé	fixed price	serviced site	*viabilisé*
quincaillerie	ironmonger's (shop)	sewage (disposal)	*assainissement*
rampe d'escalier	banisters	sill	*appui*
rangements	storage areas	situated	*situé*
realisation	to carry out agreement	skip (for rubbish)	*benne*

rebuchage	infilling (cracks)	skirting	*plinthe*
rédiger un contrat	to make (draw up) a contract	spade	*bêche*
refaire la surface	to resurface	spanner	*clé*
remise	postponement	square, out of, or not	*hors d'équerre*
rémise en état	reconditioning	staircase	*escalier*
revêtement	surface	start (of building work)	*ouverture de chantier*
revêtement de sol	floor covering	stopcock	*robinet d'arret*
robinet à flotteur	ballcock	storage areas	*rangements*
robinet d'arrêt	stopcock	storey	*étage*
robinetterie	taps and bath fittings	supply or supplier	*alimentation*
rondelle	washer	surface	*revêtement*
salle de bains	bathroom	survey (property)	*visite d'expert*
salon	sitting room	survey or surveyor	*géomètre*
scie	saw	tank	*citerne*
salle de séjour	living room	tank (septic)	*fosse septique*
situé	situated	tape (measuring)	*mètre ruban*
sol	ground	tarpaulin	*bâche*
solive de plancher	floor joist	tenure, right to	*jouissance*
solive en acier	steel joist	terrace	*terrasse*
souche	chimney stack	trader (legal and licensed)	*commerçant*
sous sol	cellar	tray (e.g. for mixing plaster)	*bac à gâcher*

terrain	grounds	tray (shower)	*bac de douche*
terrain constructible	land (building)	trowel	*truelle*
terrasse	terrace	turf (to put down)	*gazonner*
terre sol	earth (electrical)	vendor	*vendeur*
toiture	roof	veneer	*placage*
tournevis	screwdriver	wall plug	*cheville*
tout-à-l'égout	mains drainage	wall, retaining	*mur de retenue*
traveaux	work (required)	washer	*rondelle*
truelle	trowel	water supply	*alimentation en eau*
tubage	flue (metal liner)	water tank	*ballon d'eau*
tuyeu de trop-plein	overflow (pipe or drain)	wheelbarrow	*brouette*
vendeur	vendor	window	*fenêtre*
vermoulu	woodworm (holes)	window (to put in)	*poser une vitre*
viabilisé	serviced site	window (catch)	*agrafe*
vice de construction	botched building work	window, sash	*fenêtre à guillotine*
vis	screw	woodworm (holes)	*vermoulu*
visite d'expert	property survey	wool (wire)	*laine d'acier*
vitrage	glazing	work (required)	*traveaux*

Sample Projects

Throughout this section, it has been assumed that most of these items were done by a professional builder/joiner/glazer, etc. Kitchen and bathroom fittings were to be of moderate quality, not the cheapest, but certainly not the most expensive. Basic decoration provides for the materials and for the owner putting coats of paint/varnish on surfaces. Nothing has been allowed in these budgets for fittings such as shelves beyond those in kitchen cupboards. Bathroom/kitchen installation is to include some basic tiling and the bath would have a shower over it.

HOUSE 1 – HAUTE VIENNE: €11,000

Petite maison de ville à rénover. 1 pièce avec cheminée. 1er étage: 2 pièces avec cheminées. 2ème étage: 2 pièces avec cheminées. petite cour sur le côté de la maison assez grande pour une table et des chaises! pas de chauffage, ni d'évacuation sanitaire.

Translation

Small town house to renovate. 1 room with fireplace. First floor: 2 bedrooms with fireplaces. 2nd floor: 2 bedrooms with fireplaces. Small yard to side of house just right for a table and chairs. No central heating, no mains drainage.

Suggested costings for renovation:

Attention to exterior walls	€3,650
Some replastering	€1,100
Complete installation of bathroom	€2,100
Complete installation of kitchen (inc. cooker and fridge)	€7,500
Complete installation of central heating (8 radiators)	€6,500
Basic decoration	€1,400
Total	€22,250
Grand Total:	**€33,250**

HOUSE 2 – HAUTE VIENNE: €18,000

Grange non attenante à convertir dans un petit village. le toit nécessite un minimum d'attention mais malgrè tout en bon état. assez haute pour un rez de chaussée et un premier étage. jardin tout autour, et permission pour la fosse septique. jolie vue. grande ouverture déjà en place.

Translation

Detached barn for conversion in a small village. The roof needs a minimum of attention, but is basically in good condition. Floor needed for ground floor and first floor. Garden all round and permission for a septic tank. Pretty view. Large doorway already in place.

Suggested costings for renovation:

Attention to roof	€2,250
New floor to ground floor	€3,350
New floor to upper storey	€11,250
12 new windows	€7,800
Joinery/glazing to barn door	€4,250
Installation of staircase	€1,800
Complete wiring	€6,000
Construction of interior dividing walls on both floors	€10,400
Plastering (inc. materials)	€1,400
Complete installation of drainage (including septic tank)	€7,000
Complete installation of central heating (12 radiators)	€7,400
Complete installation of bathroom	€2,100
Complete installation of kitchen (inc. cooker and fridge)	€9,600
Basic decoration	€2,800
Total	€77,400
Grand Total:	**€95,400**

HOUSE 3 – LOIRE ATLANTIQUE: €146,000

20 minutes de Nantes maison en pièrre dans son hameau comprenant cuisine avec cheminée, salon, 3 chambres, buanderie, cellier, salle d'eau, WC, dépendances en pierre, terrain 1000 m² environ.

Translation

20 minutes from Nantes, a stone house in a hamlet comprising kitchen with fireplace, living room, laundry, storeroom, bathroom, separate toilet. Stone outhouses, land in the region of 1000m².

Suggested costings for renovation:

Attention to exterior walls	€ 3,700
(Some) replastering	€1,100
Complete installation of bathroom	€1,150
Complete installation of kitchen (inc. cooker and fridge)	€7,400
Complete installation of central heating (8 radiators)	€6,500
Basic decoration	€1,400
Total	€21,250
Grand Total:	**€167,250**

HOUSE 4 – LOIRE ATLANTIQUE: €183,000

Avec vue sur l'etang de … superbe longère a rénover de 120 m² au sol, four a pains, grenier amenageáble sure toute la surface. Possibilité de plus de 200 m² habitables. Le tout sur un terrain de plus de 5000 m².

Translation

With a view over … Pond, a superb longhouse to renovate. Floor area of 120m², bread oven, attic laid out over the whole area. Possibility of creating a dwelling of more than 200m². The whole is set in more than 5000m² of land.

Suggested costings for renovation:

Complete installation of central heating (8 radiators)	€5,100
Complete installation of bathroom	€1,800
Complete installation of kitchen	€7,400
Complete rewiring	€4,000
Plastering	€1,750
Construction of interior dividing walls on both floors	€7,000
8 new windows and 1 exterior door	€6,600
Basic decoration	€1,350
Total	€35,000
Grand Total:	**€218,000**

HOUSE 5 – BRITTANY: €185,407

Longère offrant de belles perspectives de rénovation sur 3000m² de terrain, 3 pièces principales, grenier, four à pains. Environnement agréable.

Translation

Longhouse offering a good prospect of renovation on 3000m² of land. 3 principal rooms, attic, bread oven. Pleasant surroundings.

Suggested costings for renovation:

Complete installation of central heating (8 radiators)	€5,100
Complete installation of bathroom	€2,000
Complete installation of kitchen	€7,400
Construction of interior walls to first floor	€3,150
Complete rewiring	€4,750
Plastering	€2,000
12 new windows and 2 exterior doors	€9,000
Basic decoration	€1,350
Total	€34,750
Grand Total:	**€220,157**

HOUSE 6 – CHARENTE MARITIME: €72,240

MAISON DE VILLAGE A MODERNISER, comprenant: RdC: Entrée, cuisine avec cheminée, séjour avec cheminée. Etage: Palier, 3 pièces. Surface de 100m². Cour en façade – Hangar attenant avec écurie. Terrain de 150m².

Translation

Village house to modernise, comprising (on the ground floor) kitchen with fireplace, living room with fireplace. First floor: landing, 3 rooms. 100m² floor area in total. Yard in front, adjoining barn with stable.

Suggested costing for renovation:

Complete installation of central heating (6 radiators)	€ 4,600
Complete installation of bathroom	€1,800
Complete installation of kitchen (inc. cooker and fridge)	€7,400
Basic decoration	€1,100
Total	€14,900
Grand Total:	**€87,140**

Plans of La Maison D'Etre

UPSTAIRS

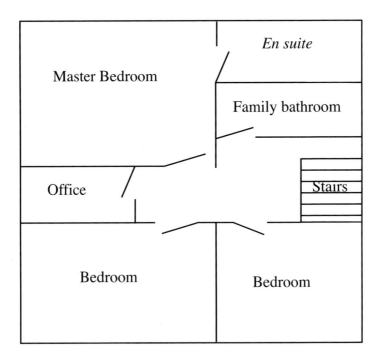

DOWNSTAIRS

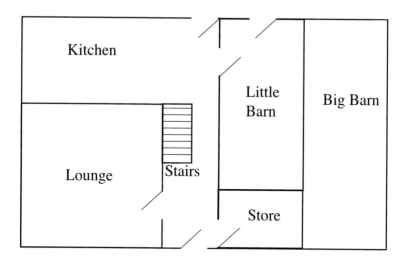

THE PLOT

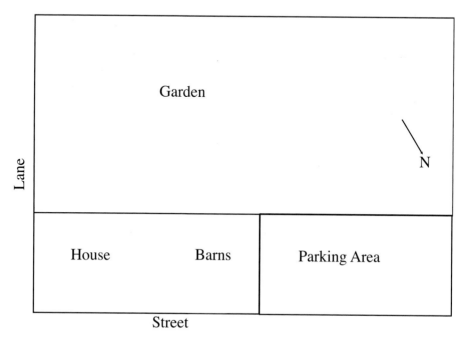

Don't get caught out when making regular foreign currency transfers

Even once you have bought your property you need to make sure that you don't forget about foreign exchange. It's highly likely that you'll need to make regular foreign currency transfers from the UK whether for mortgage payments, maintenance expenditure or transferring pensions or salaries, and you may not realise that using your bank to arrange these transfers isn't always the best option. Low exchange rates, high fees and commission charges all eat away at your money and mean that each time you use your bank you lose out. However, by using Currencies Direct's Overseas Regular Transfer Plan you can get more of your money time after time.

Exchange Rates

Your bank is likely to only offer you a tourist rate of exchange due to the small amounts being transferred. However, Currencies Direct is able to offer you a commercial rate of exchange regardless of the amount that you wish to transfer.

Transfer Charges

Most banks will typically charge between £10 and £40 for every monthly transfer. Currencies Direct is able to offer free transfers, which will save you a considerable amount of money over time.

Commission Charges

When made through a bank transfers are usually liable for a commission charge of around 2%. By using Currencies Direct you can avoid commission charges altogether.

How does it work?

It is very easy to use Currencies Direct. The first thing you need to do is open an account with them. Once this is done all you need to do is set up a direct debit with your bank and confirm with Currencies Direct how much money you would like to send and how often (monthly or quarterly). They will then take the money from your account on a specified day and once they have received the cleared funds transfer it to France at the best possible rate available.

Information provided by Currencies Direct.
www.currenciesdirect.com
Tel: 0845 389 1729
Email: *info@currenciesdirect.com*

Index